# Tick...Tick...

Hear that clock ticking? It's the countdow
and Composition Exam, and it'll be here
you have one year or one day to go, now's
your score.

D0822330

. to start maximizing

### The Test is Just a Few Months Away!

The rest of us are jealous—you're ahead of the game. But you still need to make the most of your time. Start on page 141, where we'll help you devise **year-round strategies** to make the most of your time so you'll be well-prepared for the big day.

### Actually, I Only Have a Few Weeks!

That's plenty of time for a full review. Turn to "The Main Course," where you'll find a **comprehensive guide** to the multiple-choice section and the essays, as well as **diagnostic sections** to assess your skills.

### Let's Be Honest, the Test is Tomorrow and I'm Freaking Out!

No problem. Read through the **Last-Minute Study Guide** (page 1). Then grab a pencil and take the **practice test** (page 149). Don't worry about your score—just focus on getting to know the test. Before you go to bed, go through the **Checklist for the Night Before** (page 2) and keep it close. It'll walk you through the day ahead.

Relax. Everything you need to know, you've already learned. We're just here to keep it fresh in your mind for test day.

# My Max Score

## AP ENGLISH LITERATURE AND COMPOSITION

### Maximize Your Score in Less Time

Tony Armstrong

Published by Sourcebooks, Inc.
P.O. Box 4410, Naperville, Illinois 60567-4410
(630) 961-3900
Fax: (630) 961-2168
www.sourcebooks.com

Library of Congress Cataloging-in-Publication Data

Armstrong, Tony.
    My max score AP English Literature: maximize your score in less time / by Tony Armstrong.
        p. cm.
1. English literature—Examinations—Study guides. 2. Advanced placement programs (Education)—Examinations—Study guides. I. Title.
    PR87.A76 2011
    820.76—dc22
                                        2010039351
        Printed and bound in the United States of America.
            VP 10 9 8 7 6 5 4 3 2 1

# Contents

# Acknowledgments

Big thanks to: Jan Guffin, my former boss and mentor; Ed Coleman, my current boss and colleague; Jocelyn Sisson, my best critic and collaborator; David Andrews, my editor; Tiffany, my wife; Lucy and Max, my kids; and the thousands of students who have taught me over the decades.

# Introduction

Everybody comes to an AP test from a different place. For some, it's the one AP test of their high school career, while for others it's just one of many. Some students have been focused on it all year, supplementing their classwork with extra practice at home. Other students haven't been able to devote the time they would like—perhaps other classes, extracurricular activities, after-school jobs, or other obligations have gotten in the way. Wherever you're coming from, this book can help. It's divided into three sections: a last-minute study guide to use the week before, a comprehensive review for those with more than a week to prepare, and a long-term study plan for students preparing well in advance.

Think of these sections as a suggestion rather than a rigid prescription. Feel free to pick and choose the pieces from each section that you find most helpful. If you have time, review everything—and take as many practice tests as you can.

Whether you need to have a day or a year to study, there are a few things you need to know before diving in. Let's start by getting to know the AP English Literature and Composition Exam.

## About the Exam

The AP English Literature Exam lasts for three hours and consists of two sections, a multiple-choice section and an essay section. The essay section is divided into three parts: poetry analysis, prose analysis, and a literature essay.

The multiple-choice section contains 50 to 60 questions, and you are given an hour to answer them. It contains 2 or 3 poems and 2 or 3 prose passages, each of which you must analyze before responding to the questions that follow it. There is no penalty for guessing incorrectly, so it's always better to guess than to leave an item blank.

In the poetry essay, you must write an essay that explains the author's technique in the poem, including analysis of literary devices and elements such as figurative language, structure, or tone. For the prose essay you are given a passage from a novel, short story, play, or other literary passage, and asked to analyze the passage in response to the prompt provided. The final essay asks you to choose a novel or play you have read—no short stories or nonfiction, please—and analyze it in response to the question provided.

## Scoring

The multiple-choice section is worth 45 percent of your final grade, and the three essays together are worth 55 percent.

Each essay is graded on a scale of 1 to 9, with a 9 being an exceptional essay and a 1 being incoherent, off topic, or otherwise unacceptable. These scores are combined to give you an AP grade:

5) Extremely well qualified
4) Well qualified
3) Qualified
2) Possibly qualified
1) Not recommended for AP credit

To earn a 3, a rough guide is that you will need to answer at least 60 to 65 percent of the multiple-choice questions correctly and earn at least a 5 on each essay.

## What's on the Exam

The challenge of the AP English Literature Exam is that there's not just one set of knowledge. Instead, it's a test of your ability to carefully read and analyze "imaginative literature," which refers to fictional works, plays, and poetry. Successful students must be able to interpret how writers use language to provide meaning and enjoyment for the reader, and analyze how aspects such as structure, style, and themes, as well as smaller elements such as figurative language, imagery, symbolism, and tone, come into play in a piece of writing.

There is no set reading list—in fact, the creators of the exam work hard to ensure that you haven't read the pieces that appear on the exam. The final essay asks you to use a work of literature of your own choosing to respond to the prompt, so it's a good idea to be familiar with a wide range of works that you can choose from when writing this essay.

Visit mymaxscore.com for an additional practice test for the AP English Literature and Composition Exam, as well as practice tests for other AP subjects.

# THE ESSENTIALS: A LAST-MINUTE STUDY GUIDE

Okay, so it's a night or two before the exam and you just don't feel ready. Is it time to panic? No, it's time to prepare. If you've been taking an AP English Literature class, or preparing in other ways throughout the year, then you're nearly there. All you need now is to settle your nerves, review a few strategies to refresh your mind, and line everything up for test day. It's not too late to maximize your score.

Get focused. You don't have much time, so you'll want to make the most of the time you have. Turn off all your electronics and technological gadgetry. No texting or web-surfing. Ask your family not to bother you unless it's really important. Close the door. Ready? Then let's get started.

## Review the Test-Taking Tips

Start by getting to know the test. Go over the Quick Test-Taking Tips on page 5. There are more in-depth strategies on pages 27 and 53 if you have a few nights.

## Go Over Prose and Poetry Reading

Read over the sections on how to read a prose passage and how to read a poem. You may already have your own strategies, but chances are you'll pick up something useful from reading these sections. Remember that it's not enough just to get the gist of the passages you read—you must analyze them as you read, searching for deeper meaning, and to do that it helps to annotate as you go.

## Take a Practice Exam

This is the key to your preparation. Do the practice exam on page 149 in real time. Don't take a break or look at any of the answers until you've completed the entire exam. Use the practice test as a chance to practice your skills and identify any weaknesses. If you still have time, make the most of it by reviewing the areas in which you need the most work by reading other appropriate sections in this book.

## Any Last Words?

Let's say it's the morning of the exam and for some lucky reason, you find yourself with this book. Look over the essay prompts in the practice test. Familiarizing yourself with the types of questions the essays ask will give you a head start on figuring out how to respond to them. Read the test-taking tips, go over the following checklist, and leave plenty of time for a good night's sleep.

## Checklist for the Night Before

- Put together a backpack or small bag with everything you'll need for the test. Have it ready the night before so that you can grab it and go, knowing you're properly equipped. Here is what you might put inside:
    - Several pencils, a good eraser (test it first to make sure it erases without marking the paper), and several black or blue pens. Use erasable pens if you want, but make sure they don't smudge.

- A small, easy to eat snack. Avoid chocolate, which could melt and get all over your hands and your desk. Avoid nuts, which could trigger allergies in other testers. An energy bar, an easy-to-eat piece of fruit, or some crackers would be good choices.

- A bottle of water. Avoid drinks with sugar or caffeine. You may think they'll give you energy, but they're more likely to make you jittery.

- Don't stay up all night studying. Get a good night's sleep so you will be alert and ready for the test.

- Eat a light but satisfying meal before the test. Protein-rich foods like eggs, nuts, and yogurt are a good choice. Don't eat too heavily—you don't want to be sleepy or uncomfortably full. If you must have coffee, don't overdo it.

- Dress in layers. You want to be able to adjust if the testing room is too warm or too cool. Wear comfortable clothes.

### Test Day

- Don't bring anything you don't need. Cell phones, pagers, and anything else that might let you communicate outside the test room will be prohibited.

- Do bring a photo ID and your school code.

- Wear or bring a watch. If your watch has any alarms, buzzers, or beepers, turn them off.

Once you get to the testing room, take a few deep breaths and relax. Remind yourself that you're well prepared. It's natural to be nervous. Channel your nervousness into alertness and energy for the long test ahead. When the test begins, set all worries aside. You've done all you can to prepare, and now it's time to make that preparation pay off!

# Quick Test-Taking Tips

---

## Multiple-Choice Tips

---

With 50 to 60 questions to answer in an hour, the multiple-choice section tends to whiz by, but with the right strategies in place, you can make the most of that precious time to maximize your score. The key is to find and answer the questions you know, and make a best guess on the questions you don't. For the extended version of these strategies, head to page 27. But assuming you don't have time for that, let's get started.

## Tip 1: Plan Your Attack

Flip through the booklet to see how many passages and how many question are on the test. This rundown will help you: a) keep track of what's coming up next, and b) pace yourself for the first hour.

As you look through, glance over the passages and decide which ones you want to read first. You might prefer to begin with the passage that looks easiest, or the form (poetry or prose) that you are most comfortable with. If you do jump around, be sure you're filling in the correct ovals on your answer sheet!

## Tip 2: Scan, Read, and Annotate

Here's how to approach your reading of each passage.

1. Scan the passage to get the gist of it.

2. Scan the question stems (not the answer choices) to see what they are asking about in the passage.

3. Go back and read the passage more carefully, annotating it as you go. Jot down anything you think is particularly meaningful, strange, repetitive, or revealing. Think as you read.

4. Begin answering the questions.

## Tip 3: The "Hourglass" Format

Know which types of questions to expect. The questions at the beginning and end are likely to be more general questions about the passage as a whole. The questions in the middle will probably refer to specific sections of the passage, in chronological order.

## Tip 4: Check the Stem's Boundaries

Check the phrasing of the question to see what lines you are restricted to, if any. Stay within those boundaries when choosing your answer. You can quickly eliminate answer choices that deal with material from another part of the passage.

## Tip 5: Watch for Context

Isolating a word or phrase from its context may drastically alter its meaning. Be sure to review the text immediately before or after the word or phrase in context so you are clear on the meaning that is intended.

## Tip 6: Not All Opinions Are Equal

Some answers are partially correct, but still can't be justified as the *best* answer. Check all the answers before you choose one. A may seem correct at first, but the phrasing of E could make it the better answer.

## Tip 7: Answer Every Question

There's no longer any penalty for an incorrect question, so it pays to answer every question. If you run out of time and can't get to a question, fill something in anyway—you may just get lucky!

---

## Essay Tips

---

For the essay section, you will have two hours to write three essays, an average of 40 minutes per essay. Here's how to make the most of that time.

## Tip 1: Scan the Section and Organize Your Time

The first essay asks you to analyze a poem. The second essay asks you to analyze an excerpt from a piece of fiction, while the third essay asks you to discuss a major work such as a novel or play. You don't have to address the essays in their prescribed order. If you want to write the third essay first because it seems the easiest or most difficult, you may do so. If you tackle the "easiest" essay first, try to finish it in less than 40 minutes so you have more time to devote to the more difficult essays.

## Tip 2: Plan Before You Write

a) Annotate the poem or prose excerpt before you write about it. Jot down your thoughts in the margins and underline words or phrases that particularly stand out.

b) Analyze the prompt before you write. Make sure that you understand everything it is asking, and that your response responds to it directly.

## Tip 3: Write a Balanced Introduction

a) The introduction should not be too abrupt, nor should it be self-indulgent and rambling.

b) The introduction should be wholly focused on the text: don't delve into history, personal anecdotes, or hypothetical situations.

c) A brief summary of the work you are discussing that leads into your analytical thesis is the most direct introduction you can write, and often the most effective.

d) Funnel the introduction down to the thesis, but don't spend time summarizing all the arguments you will make in the essay.

## Tip 4: Make Your Examples Appropriate, Varied, and Original

a) Your examples must come from the text; you must use the appropriate text for each point.

b) If your examples keep proving the very same point, you don't have enough variety; each example should take a slightly different "spin" on your thesis.

c) If you choose predictable examples to prove your thesis, your essay will seem too ordinary and not strong enough to earn a top score.

## Tip 5: Organize Your Points Climactically

Save the most important or most unusual example for the end of your essay's body. Doing so will help lead you into a new idea for your conclusion.

## Tip 6: Don't Discuss the Reader

Your essay should focus on text analysis, not guessing how a hypothetical reader will respond to the text. If you spend time discussing the way the reader will respond, you risk sounding as if you don't know what is happening in the text.

## Tip 7: Conclude by Reviewing and Re-Viewing

Don't just summarize your points in your conclusion. Use the conclusion to reveal a new idea about the text, show the passage in a new light, or extend your argument.

## Tip 8: "Translate" the Poem

When analyzing the poem, follow these steps to help understand it:

a) Look for the sentences. The end of a line in a poem does not necessarily mean the end of a sentence. Pay attention to the poem's punctuation or lack thereof. Finding the complete sentences will help you find the poem's complete ideas.

b) Reorder sentences into natural syntax, if necessary. Many times, a poem will re-order the natural syntax or phrasing of a sentence to place emphasis on particular words. For the sake of clarification, you can reshuffle the words of a line in your mind to find their standard phrasing.

c) Translate from King James English, if necessary. See page 80 for translations of common Elizabethan words.

## Tip 9: In the Prose Passage, Beware of Satire

Satire is often written with a serious, sincere tone. If your narrator or speaker sounds serious, but is describing an idea or character that seems a bit "off," you may be dealing with satire.

## Tip 10: In the Third Essay, Choose Wisely

The third question always provides a list of recommended works deemed appropriate for the prompt. If you use the list, choose a work that:

- you know well but can remain emotionally detached from (a deep love or hatred of a work can ruin your objectivity)

- is not the most obvious choice on the list (your AP reader is bound to score dozens of essays dealing with the obvious choice on the list, so a predictable choice is not likely to stand out)

You are not obligated to choose a work from the recommended list, but if you opt for another piece of literature, make certain it is substantive, has literary merit, and applies well to the prompt.

# One Way to Read a Passage

**M**any readers do not understand what it means to read a text closely. Some read for pleasure or entertainment. They can appreciate a text while they read, even judge it as good or bad. Others will skim a passage and may be able to relate its general ideas, but can't explain to you how the work creates meaning. To do well on the AP Literature Exam, however, requires "close reading."

To read closely is to relate the text to itself, to other texts, to ourselves, and to the exam's multiple-choice items. The best way to see these relationships is to engage the text by annotating it. Let's try some initial experiments with close reading of a play excerpt.

What follows is an excerpt from a play. Many students love to read plays because these works are driven by dialogue. Without being slowed down by a narrator's descriptions, the reader can enjoy the characterization more readily, skim the text more easily, and finish it more quickly than other passages. In other words, a play is a prime candidate for *not* being read closely.

Therefore, let's do the unusual and subject the text to a close reading. As you move through it, pause and take note when one of the following happens:

a) The text makes a personal connection with you or with another text; the connection may help you understand something unexpected about the passage.

b)  A later portion of the text ties in with an earlier portion; it is always good to see the interrelationships of a literary piece so that you can view it as a unified whole.

c)  The text raises a question in your mind; noting a temporary confusion early in the passage can lead to a greater clarity later.

The numbers in parentheses indicate where a student might have made a note. Just know that these are not the only places to read closely. Your results may vary.

[In the following passage, two gentlewomen discuss the dynamics of male-female relationships]

[Enter Mrs. Fainall and Mrs. Marwood]

**Mrs. Fain**. Ay, ay, dear Marwood, if we will be happy, we must find the means in ourselves, and among ourselves. Men are ever in extremes, either doting or averse. While they are lovers, if they have fire and sense, their jealousies are insupportable; and when they cease to love (we ought to think at least) they loathe (1); they look upon us with horror and distaste; they meet us like the ghosts of what we were, and as from such, fly from us.

**Mrs. Mar**. True, 'tis an unhappy circumstance of life, that love should ever die before us; and that the man so often should outlive the lover. But say what you will, 'tis better to be left than never to have been loved. To pass our youth in dull indifference, to refuse the sweets of life because they once must leave us, is as preposterous as to wish to have been born old, because we one day must be old. For my part, my youth may wear and waste, but it shall never rust (2) in my possession.

**Mrs. Fain.** Then it seems you dissemble an aversion to mankind only in compliance to my mother's humour.[1]

---

1    *my mother's humourhs*: Mrs. Fainall's mother has suffered a recent romantic disappointment and as a result, distrusts all men.

**Mrs. Mar.** Certainly. To be free; I have no taste of those insipid dry discourses, with which our sex of force must entertain themselves, apart from men. We may affect endearments to each other, profess eternal friendships, and seem to dote like lovers; but 'tis not in our natures long to persevere. Love will resume his empire in our breasts, (3) and every heart, or soon or late, receive and readmit him as its lawful tyrant.

**Mrs. Fain.** Bless me, how have I been deceived! Why, you profess a libertine.

**Mrs. Mar.** You see my friendship by my freedom. (4) Come, be as sincere, acknowledge that your sentiments agree with mine.

**Mrs. Fain.** Never. (5)

**Mrs. Mar.** You hate mankind?

**Mrs. Fain.** Heartily, inveterately.

**Mrs. Mar.** Your husband?

**Mrs. Fain.** Most transcendently; ay, though I say it, meritoriously.

**Mrs. Mar.** Give me your hand upon it.

**Mrs. Fain.** There.

**Mrs. Mar.** I join with you; what I have said has been to try you.

**Mrs. Fain.** Is it possible? Dost thou hate those vipers, men? (6)

**Mrs. Mar.** I have done hating 'em, and am now come to despise 'em; the next thing I have to do, is eternally to forget 'em (7)

**Mrs. Fain.** There spoke the spirit of an Amazon, a Penthesilea.[2]

**Mrs. Mar.** And yet I am thinking sometimes to carry my aversion further.

**Mrs. Fain.** How?

**Mrs. Mar.** Faith, by marrying; (8) if I could not but find one that loved me very well, and would be thoroughly sensible of ill usage, I think I should do myself the violence of undergoing the ceremony.

**Mrs. Fain.** You would not make him a cuckold?[3]

**Mrs. Mar.** No; but I'd make him believe I did, and that's as bad.

**Mrs. Fain.** Why had not you as good do it?

---

2    *Penthesilea*: Queen of the Amazons, killed by Achilles in the Trojan War.

3    *cuckold*: one whose wife is cheating on him.

**Mrs. Mar.** Oh, if he should ever discover it, he would then know the worst, and be out of his pain; but I would have him ever to continue upon the rack of fear and jealousy. (9)

**Mrs. Fain.** Ingenious mischief!

(1700)

If we were to read the passage merely for enjoyment, we might dismiss these two characters as a couple of crazy but amusing women.

Skimming the excerpt, we could summarize the situation in this way: the two characters harbor secret thoughts about men, but are willing to trust each other with these secrets.

If we are just trying to get the passage over with, we might be put off by the 18th century patterns of speech.

None of these approaches, however, provide the kind of close reading necessary to survive the AP Literature Exam. Consider the notes below and see how they demonstrate not only a greater engagement with the text, but also how they reveal a possible pattern emerging in the excerpt.

(1) patterns of opposites; "doting/averse," "love/loathe"—why?

(2) difference between "wear and waste" (active) and rust (inactive)

(3) when women are close, love is not reigning; love back on the throne, women prefer men to other women…Marwood is like that friend that doesn't call other friends when she's in love

(4) freedom = true feelings

(5) conflict—Fainall disagrees with Marwood

(6) No, wait. Marwood agrees with Fainall: men stink; can Marwood be trusted? Has she been as "free" as she says?

(7) Why the "'em's"? Marwood alters speech pattern to reflect strong negative feelings?

(8) purpose of marriage seems paradoxical; marry to make them doubt your faithfulness

(9) opposites and paradoxes reflect sneakiness of these deceitful women; opposites = duality…duality = two-faced…lying, covering up

In these notes, you can see an emerging sense of unity in the construction of the scene. Close reading has led to a discovery of a duality motif.

When you read a passage in the exam, your notes may be even less detailed than these. The key is to be thinking about what's happening in the passage as you read it, and jotting down whatever strikes you as surprising or revealing.

# One Way to Read a Poem

Poetry may be the most complex of all literary genres. A poem is like a black hole of meaning—it is a compact and dense creation that has the power to alter space and time.

In this section, we are going to suggest one method for analyzing a poem, but keep in mind the following points:

1. This study method is not the alpha and omega of study methods, but it is a good way to see how different aspects of a poem coalesce into a unified whole.

2. The method shown here will be useful for annotating poetry on both the multiple-choice section of the exam and the first essay, which asks you to discuss a poem.

3. This method can also be applied to prose passages that appear on the test.

4. Outside the context of an exam, a poem should not just be studied, but appreciated; after you take the AP Literature Exam, go read some poetry just for pleasure or enlightenment.

With those points in mind, let's get started.

Think of reading a poem as if it were a dive into a cold ocean. The experience can be invigorating, refreshing, even a little scary, but the more often you dive in and the longer you stay in, the more familiar and comfortable you'll be with the waves and currents, until you feel as if you are actually part of the water. To achieve this kind of ease with a poem, you need to take at least four "D.I.P.S." in it; in other words, you should annotate four different elements of the poem to see how they independently and interactively create meaning in the text.

In the first dip, you look at the poem's DICTION, or its word choice. To relieve yourself of the stress of trying to understand everything at once, just underline the words in the poem that stand out to you, for whatever reason. Maybe you like the way they sound, or they cause you to ask questions, or you think they are particularly appropriate. About 5 to 7 words would be adequate for this first step. We'll use a poem by William Wordsworth to demonstrate:

### The Tables Turned

Up! up! my Friend, and quit your books;
Or surely you'll grow double:
Up! up! my Friend, and clear your looks;
Why all this toil and trouble?

5   The sun, above the mountain's head,
A freshening lustre mellow
Through all the long green fields has spread,
His first sweet evening yellow.

Books! 'tis a dull and endless strife:
10 Come, hear the woodland linnet,
How sweet his music! on my life,
There's more of wisdom in it.

And hark! how blithe the throstle sings!
He, too, is no mean preacher:
15 Come forth into the light of things,
Let Nature be your teacher.

She has a world of ready wealth,

Our minds and hearts to bless

Spontaneous wisdom breathed by health,

20 Truth breathed by cheerfulness.


One impulse from a vernal wood

May teach you more of man,

Of moral evil and of good,

Than all the <u>sages</u> can.


25 Sweet is the lore which Nature brings;

Our meddling intellect

Mis-shapes the beauteous forms of things:

We murder to dissect.


Enough of Science and of Art;

30 Close up those <u>barren</u> leaves;

Come forth, and bring with you a heart

That watches and receives.


We underlined the following words: quit, freshening, dull, throstle, teacher, sages, barren. However, some others may have caught your eye. But no matter: the point here is that after noticing a series of words throughout the text, you try to find a shared *tone* among them—what do they reveal about the speaker's attitude toward his subject?

The word *quit* sounds more final than *leave*, and what is it that we are supposed to quit? Books.

*Freshening* is a sharp contrast to *dull*. The word *freshening* pertains to a natural environment, while *dull* relates to books, which the speaker has just told us to abandon.

*Throstle* is unfamiliar, as is *linnet*, which didn't make our list, but they both must be kinds of birds, since they sing and make music in nature.

Speaking of nature, we notice that nature is talked about as a female "teacher" in the poem, and that she is superior to human "sages," or wise men.

Our last word, *barren*, matches up with the word *dull* in line 9. In the last stanza, leaves are barren. This image seems to go against the positive view of nature in this work, but we are told to close up these leaves after the speaker says "Enough of Science and of Art" (line 29). So, the leaves must be pages of books about science and art.

When we look for a tonal pattern in our DICTION dip, we are trying to find some emotional quality that governs the work, an emotion that goes beyond mere happiness or sadness. If we look at the relationship among these words in their context, we might determine that the speaker has an *exhorting* or *admonishing* tone. He is urging us to take action, to enter into nature, and advising us that book knowledge is inferior to the simple experience of nature.

Next, after we establish tone in our DICTION dip, we go to the "I" of the D.I.P.S. process: IMAGERY. Look for two to four excerpts in the poem that appeal to the senses or use figurative language:

> Up! up! my Friend, and quit your books;
> Or surely you'll grow double:
> Up! up! my Friend, and clear your looks;
> Why all this toil and trouble?
>
> 5  The sun, above the mountain's head,
>    A freshening lustre mellow
>    Through all the long green fields has spread,
>    His first sweet evening yellow.
>
> Books! 'tis a dull and endless strife:
> 10 Come, hear the woodland linnet,
>    How sweet his music! on my life,
>    There's more of wisdom in it.
>
> And hark! how blithe the throstle sings!
> He, too, is no mean preacher:
> 15 Come forth into the light of things,
>    Let Nature be your Teacher.

She has a world of ready wealth,

Our minds and hearts to bless

Spontaneous wisdom breathed by health,

20  Truth breathed by cheerfulness.


One impulse from a vernal wood

May teach you more of man,

Of moral evil and of good,

Than all the sages can.


25  Sweet is the lore which Nature brings;

<u>Our meddling intellect</u>

<u>Mis-shapes the beauteous forms of things:</u>

<u>We murder to dissect.</u>


Enough of Science and of Art;

30  Close up those barren leaves;

Come forth, and bring with you a heart

That watches and receives.


The first image we have selected occurs in the second stanza. Here, the sun is personified, given a male gender, and not seen simply shining or growing dim in the evening, but rather "spreading" his "yellow" across the green fields. The image makes the sun sound influential and omnipresent.

The throstle in lines 13–14 sings a song, but is referred to by the speaker as a "preacher." The song, then, could be likened to a sermon, as if there is something spiritual to learn from it.

Our final selected image appears in lines 26–28, and rather than focusing on nature, this one describes humankind, and certainly in unkind terms. People have intellect, but it is "meddling," a busybody that ruins the beauty of the natural world. We are also indirectly compared to surgeons who, in attempting to study Nature, actually murder it in dissection.

The point of the IMAGERY dip is twofold. First, we want to go beyond the text's tone and begin to see more concretely what its main ideas are. Secondly, we want to tie the imagery in to the work's diction, to view the text as unified and consistent. To that end, we would say that in both diction and imagery, the poem reveals a sharp division between the rejuvenating power of nature and the flawed reasoning of humans. We may think we are intelligent, but nature is really the one that can teach us what is truly important.

The third step in the D.I.P.S. process is the "P": PATTERN. There are actually four different patterns you can keep an eye out for when annotating a text. If we go back to our ocean analogy, you could think of the pattern as a friendly killer whale, or **ORCA,** that shows up while you are frolicking among the waves of the text:

**O**pposites

**R**epetitions

**C**omparisons

**A**nomalies

The poem seems to suggest that humans and nature are **O**pposites in the way that we pursue knowledge: people use artificial means—books—to become learners, while nature uses, well, natural means—such as sunsets, birds, and the "vernal wood" (line 21)—to be a sort of "teacher."

As for exact **R**epetitions, the word "Nature" appears a couple of times in the poem. In lines 16 and 25, Nature is a bearer of knowledge, an educator. On the other hand, whenever the word "books" is repeated in the poem, we are to understand that they are obtuse, even dangerous (in the last stanza), and should be abandoned for Nature.

**C**omparisons are similar to Repetitions, but not as exact in language. One could look at the linnet, the throstle, and the vernal wood of the poem and see that they are all acting in a *comparative* fashion: as agents of Nature, they are there to teach, to make available a kind of education that is superior to book learning or mortal sages.

Finally, **A**nomalies are pattern breakers that could help us see subtle alterations in our original assertions about the text. Take, for instance, the sun image in the second stanza. Like the birds and the vernal wood, the sun is a manifestation of Nature's teaching; it spreads its yellow color across the world. What is paradoxical about this coloring is that it occurs during a sunset, when we would normally notice orange and red hues from the sun. Then wouldn't a sunset imply a weakening power, and wouldn't the sun be behaving differently from the birds and the woods, who inspire humankind? Not so. This setting sun is "freshening" the "green fields," more like a sunrise. Even as the sun sets, it has the power to rejuvenate. The poem remains consistent with itself.

The purpose of the PATTERN dip is to further the connections we have started to make between the DICTION and IMAGERY of the poem. Diction and imagery, however, are more rudimentary elements than patterns. They rarely hold up as discussion items in a literary essay because they are so basic. You should let them lead you to discovering the patterns in the text, which encompass more and allow for more integrated discussion in an essay.

The last part of the D.I.P.S. includes a look at the text's STRUCTURE: in the case of a poem, do we have an open (free verse, unrhymed, unmetered) form or a closed form (metered, possibly rhymed)? In either case, how does the structure reflect what is happening in the work?

Wordsworth's "The Tables Turned" is a closed form, more specifically a ballad, that employs four-line stanzas written in an ABCB rhyme scheme with the unrhymed lines having an iambic tetrameter cadence and the rhyming lines following iambic trimeter. If that description sounds like gobbledygook, then just focus on this question: in a poem that encourages us to abandon artificial knowledge and book learning, why wouldn't Wordsworth use an open form, which would mimic the free thinking and break with tradition that he is encouraging? Doesn't a closed form like a ballad sound "sing-songy"? Don't its rules and boundaries go against what the poem believes about the power of Nature?

We can defend the poem's closed form this way: the work assumes that you haven't yet "quit your books." Each stanza is trying to convince you that human knowledge is full of error and that Nature's teachings are superior to our puny intellect. Perhaps, if you were already out in the vernal wood, basking in the yellow sunshine of evening and listening to the throstle and linnet, the poem would be better written as an open form. But for now, you haven't yet closed the "barren leaves" of your textbooks, and in a sense, the poem is speaking in an orderly way to condescend to your inferior way of thinking…until you get out there and listen to Mother Nature.

We save the STRUCTURE discussion for last because the other dips deal more with content. The STRUCTURE step goes beyond content to examine how the form of the text also reflects the same meaning that has been consistently developed among the diction, imagery and patterns of the work. STRUCTURE is the final puzzle piece to see how interrelated the elements of the text truly are.

As you move through a work in either the multiple-choice or essay portions of the AP Literature Exam, addressing these four areas of diction, imagery, pattern, and structure will help to make an unfamiliar work more familiar. More importantly, the D.I.P.S. process will reveal just how integrated and consistent a text is, so that you can answer almost any question about it, or formulate an insightful and thorough essay discussing it.

# THE MAIN COURSE: COMPREHENSIVE STRATEGIES AND REVIEW

If you have a few weeks to go before the exam, there's plenty of time to brush up on your skills. Here's a plan of what you can do to prepare in the weeks ahead.

- Start by taking a practice test to get used to the exam and the questions asked. As you go through the answers, note any areas of weakness. Read the answers and their explanations. The explanations to the answers are helpful in a variety of ways. Even if you have answered a question correctly, you might not know why it is correct. If you missed a question, you will want to know why so you can avoid doing so in the future.

- Work your way through the Multiple-Choice and Essay Strategies sections to learn the best ways to approach the exam.

- Work through the mini-diagnostic sections to put the strategies into action and pinpoint areas where you need more practice.

- If you have difficulty with reading and analyzing prose or poetry, read over the tips on pages 11 and 17.

- Go over the glossary of terms on page 121. If any terms give you particular trouble, write them down on flash cards and quiz yourself on them until you know them.

- Take at least one more practice test before test day. You can find a free practice test online at www.mymaxscore.com/aptests.

- A night or two before the test, go over the Last-Minute Study Guide on page 1 for a refresher on test-taking tips. Do everything on the checklist on page 2.

- Pack your materials for the next day, get a good night's sleep, and you'll be ready to maximize your score.

# Multiple-Choice Strategies

In this section, you will find a variety of strategies for succeeding on the AP Literature and Composition Exam. If you are picking up this study guide the night before the test and you want the "quick and dirty" version of these strategies, go back to the quick test-taking tips in the previous section.

## Strategy 1. Pace Yourself: Read, Skim, Annotate

Usually, you will find around 55 multiple-choice questions on the AP Literature Exam. The idea is that, if you have three hours to take the whole test, you are basically allotted two hours to write three essays and only one hour to answer these 55 questions. That's a little over one minute per question, right?

Well, now, wait a second. If you consider the time that it takes to read the four or five passages that these 55 questions cover, suddenly you see that you have even less time for answering questions. Then, when you add in the time necessary for annotating the passages, your time seems even more reduced. No need to panic, however. Just follow these simple guidelines, and you will maximize your performance on the test.

First, read the passage briskly. Whether you are examining a poem, a passage from a story or novel, or even an excerpt from a play (which only makes the occasional appearance on the test), move your eyes quickly over the words. Don't linger over unfamiliar vocabulary or complicated sentences. The purpose of this initial reading should be to get the gist of the passage, enough to let the questions help you break down the meaning of the sentences later. Those unfamiliar words and confusing sentences may seem clearer once you read the questions—or they may not relate to any questions at all.

The next step is to look at the questions coming after the passage. Notice how many are in the set. Are there 12 or fewer? Then the test makers are probably considering this passage to be relatively light. Are there 14 or more questions? Then this excerpt is going to be a little denser; we may have to rely a bit more on the questions to carry us through. Next, skim the questions themselves. Don't bother going through the answers. Just look at the question stems, the parts of the questions that lead into the answers. By looking over the stems, we are trying to find out what the set wants us to know about the passage. Are we supposed to focus mainly on plot, characterization, theme, style, tone? More than likely, the questions will cover a range of these literary elements, but often the set will lean toward one or two.

Next, go back and address the passage again. This time, you are well-equipped. Not only do you have a general understanding of the passage, but you also know what the questions are going to ask you. The key in this next reading is to annotate the passage. Underline the words and phrases that seem most pertinent to the questions. Where do you see interconnections in the text? Draw arrows that make these connections more explicit. What ideas are evoked in the text? Make brief marginal notes to indicate these ideas. At the bottom of the text, sum up a major idea in the passage.

This process may seem long, but in reality it should take no more than 5 to 6 minutes per passage to complete: perhaps 1½ to 2 minutes for the quick read, one minute for the question scan and 2 to 3 minutes for the annotated reading. You should then have about 30 seconds to answer each question, and 30 seconds is a lot longer than you might think, especially when you have already read the question. Give our method a shot on the practice exam that appears later in this book.

Many students claim that they don't need a lot of preparation for a passage exam like the AP Literature test. These students say that all they need to do is answer the questions and they do just fine. If "just fine" means a "5" on the test, then they are right and do not need our guidance. If they are scoring anything less than a "5," then they might consider our recommendations. As for you, if you still think this read/skim/annotate approach is a little elaborate, practice exams are a great place to experiment. You may find that what works best for you is a simple annotation, or a combination of reading and looking over the questions before you begin answering. But in any case our foremost advice is to attempt this read/skim/annotate system, and by no means should you start answering questions blindly without even giving the passage a once-over.

## Strategy 2: Watch for the "Hourglass"

You may not believe it, but it's the truth: a set of multiple-choice questions on the AP Literature Exam is designed *to teach a passage* to you. Contrary to the image of test makers who gleefully devise volatile questions intended to blow up in the faces of students, the folks at the College Board and the Educational Testing Service want you to do well on the exam. They also want you to be a discerning reader, someone who can distinguish the correct answer from the "almost correct" answer. The next step in becoming that wary test taker is to be familiar with the format of the questions in any passage set.

As noted earlier, any passage you see on the test could feature between 10 and 16 questions, give or take a few. However, these questions are not haphazardly thrown together. They are, in fact, thoughtfully organized to be both invitational and insightful. For instance, you will notice that the first question tends to ask something general about the passage; perhaps the intent is to test your understanding of the passage's tone or the chief motivation of a character. The idea is to get you to think broadly—but not yet too deeply—about what you have just read, to begin letting it jell in your mind. Then the more specific questions follow. You will see as you move through the set that not only do these items run chronologically through the passage, but one question can naturally feed into the next. In a sense, the set is walking along with you on the reading journey, trying to get you to notice certain features of the textual landscape until, at the end, the last questions are once more asking you to take in the whole vista of the passage, to assemble all the smaller questions that have come before into grander questions of theme, development, and synthesis.

The question sets often follow a familiar pattern. You might call it an "hourglass" format: there are broad questions at the top, narrower chronological questions in the middle, and broad closing questions at the end.

## Strategy 3: Know the Question Types

Let's look at the following poem (actually, a song lyric) written by the Romanticist Percy Bysshe Shelley around 1820, titled "To the Men of England." He is responding to the infamous Peterloo Massacre, during which peaceful, pro-union demonstrators were gunned down by some anxious yeomen.

> Men of England, wherefore plough
> For the lords who lay ye low?
> Wherefore weave with toil and care
> The rich robes your tyrants wear?
>
> 5  Wherefore feed and clothe and save,
> From the cradle to the grave,
> Those ungrateful drones[1] who would
> Drain your sweat—nay, drink your blood?

---

1.    *drones:* nonfunctioning bees, as opposed to worker bees.

Wherefore, Bees of England, forge
10 Many a weapon, chain, and scourge,
   That these stingless drones may spoil
   The forced produce of your toil?

   Have ye leisure, comfort, calm,
   Shelter, food, love's gentle balm?
15 Or what is it ye buy so dear
   With your pain and with your fear?

   The seed ye sow another reaps;
   The wealth ye find another keeps;
   The robes ye weave another wears;
20 The arms ye forge another bears.

   Sow seed, –but let no tyrant reap;
   Find wealth, –let no imposter heap;
   Weave robes, –let not the idle wear;
   Forge arms, in your defence to bear.

25 Shrink to your cellars, holes, and cells;
   In halls ye deck another dwells.
   Why shake the chains ye wrought? Ye see
   The steel ye tempered glance on ye.

   With plough and spade and hoe and loom,
30 Trace your grave, and build your tomb,
   And weave your winding-sheet², till fair
   England be your sepulchre!

Below, you will find a typical twelve-question set analyzing the poem. Try answering each question yourself, then read the correct answer and the commentary that follows, which shows how to select the right answer for each question.

---

2.    *winding-sheet*: shroud, burial wrap.

1.   The poem's purpose is to

    A.   exhort

    B.   honor

    C.   apologize

    D.   entertain

    E.   mollify

Notice here that the question has a broad perspective. You are being asked to consider the poem as a whole. In this sense, Question 1 is behaving like a typical introductory item.

Answer A is correct because the poem is urging its readers to take action, not as they have in the past—for the wealthy of England—but for themselves. The sixth stanza (lines 21–24) makes this point especially obvious.

2.   The "lords" of line 2 are best described as

    A.   generous and understanding

    B.   intelligent and mighty

    C.   weak and cowardly

    D.   cruel and sadistic

    E.   dominant and debasing

Now, we shift to more specific test items. Question 2 is asking you to base an interpretation of the "lords" on your general reading of the text. The item is not as broad as Question 1, but it still requires you to go through a good number of stanzas before you can select the appropriate answer. Because you have to find a syntactical pattern in the text to understand how the lords are being portrayed, we would call Question 2 a "reasoning and inference" item. Also, keep in mind that the question was based on an early portion of the poem; so, indeed, the set is moving chronologically through the passage.

One can see that the lords are "dominant and debasing" (E) fairly easily in this poem. The men of England labor, but all that they produce is forcibly turned over to the lords (see stanza 3, especially line 12); thus, the lords dominate the men. Line 2 itself points out the debasement by the lords, as they "lay low" the men of England.

3.   The word "nay" in line 8 creates a transition that

    A.   demonstrates the speaker's lack of reliability
    B.   shows the unpredictability of the "drones" (line 7)
    C.   intensifies the effect of the "drones" (line 7)
    D.   illustrates the uncertainty of the time period
    E.   predicts the threat of the "Bees" (line 9)

Question 3 concentrates on a single word, but looks at its function rather than on its meaning. Therefore, we would place this item in the category of "organization" questions, those that want you to see the necessity of appropriate transitions and effective organizational strategies.

In essence, the speaker in the poem is correcting himself in line 8. He starts by saying that the men of England are drained of their sweat, so the work that they do is physically taxing. But the "nay" in the middle of the line implies that the speaker has not gone far enough. The dashes surrounding the "nay" indicate pauses that connote further consideration; then, the speaker comes up with an image of greater intensity: it would be bad enough if the sweat were forced out of England's laborers, but to have their blood drained and *drunk* by the upper classes? Shelley is making the wealthy out to be social vampires. The "nay" signals this magnification of evil. Thus, answer C is correct.

4.   All of the following could be said about the "Bees of England" image (line 9) EXCEPT THAT

    A.   it renames the "Men of England" (line 1)
    B.   it contrasts with the images of lines 7 & 11
    C.   it does not envision the workers as a collective
    D.   it refers to the diligence of the lower classes
    E.   it does not coincide metaphorically with the verb "forge" (line 9)

Oh, the "EXCEPT THAT" question. It's not fun. It makes you work a little harder for your answer. Basically, we have another "reasoning and inference" situation here, but in this instance, you have to recognize four of the answers as being plausible; it's your job to choose which one of the answers could not work in the context of the poem.

So, does A work? Yes. The "Bees of England" are addressed the same as the "Men of England": they are being spoken to as workers. The lords of England are the ineffectual drones of society, a contrast to the working bees, so B seems possible.

The word *diligence* implies that the bees/men are hardworking, and the poem sees them as nothing but diligent, so D could be right. And the word "forge" in line 9 pertains to an action found in a blacksmith's shop rather than a beehive, so the bee metaphor does not sync well with this verb and E is another reasonable answer.

We are then left with C, which claims that the image of bees is not a collective one. Yet the men of England seem to be performing the same operations: weaving, forging, sowing, and so on. They are a collective. It is the lords who stand apart from this labor, who are not part of the group. So, with an EXCEPT THAT item, we choose the answer which is wrong, and C is clearly wrong.

For another fun kind of EXCEPT question, go to Question 23 on Mini-Diagnostic, Section II.

5. The purpose of the fifth stanza (lines 17–20) is most likely to

    A. comfort the workers in a time of despair
    B. explain the ideal purpose of the workers' labor
    C. continue the "bees of England" image in line 9
    D. present an idea that has not yet been introduced in the poem
    E. anticipate and then dismiss a response to the questions in lines 13–16

Rather than deal with a single word or phrase, the set is now asking you to examine an entire stanza in the context of the poem. You might characterize Question 5 as a "rhetorical strategies" item, since it is asking the intended function of the lines.

E is correct because lines 13–16 ask a series of questions which lines 17–20 seem to answer. If I am a laborer who endures pain and fear from the upper classes, what would make me put up with such treatment? I could respond that I am allowed to farm, to run a small business, to make clothing, and to forge weapons. But the speaker reminds me in lines 17–20 that my labor only benefits those above me: they eat my food, seize my profits, wear my clothing, and wield my weapons. There is then no comfort for me, and no good reason why I should tolerate such abuse.

6. In relation to the fifth stanza, the purpose of the sixth stanza (lines 21–24) is most likely to

   A. suggest different training for the workers
   B. change the workers' focus
   C. warn the workers of their doom
   D. separate the cooperative and uncooperative workers
   E. force the workers to unite

Do you see what we mean about walking you through the journey of the passage? As the questions proceed chronologically, they very rarely want you to think about segments of the text in isolation from each other. Rather, considering one part of the poem *in relation to some other part*, you can create more resonant meaning in the passage. By the end of the question set, you will understand the text better because you have been asked to get the poem to talk to itself.

The sixth stanza of the poem exhorts the men of England to continue working: to sow, acquire, weave, and forge as they have done, but to keep the products of their labor out of the hands of the wealthy. In fact, line 24 encourages the men to keep the arms they create for themselves, presumably to defend against the upper classes. Thus, this stanza changes the focus of the workers in the previous stanza; lines 16–20 have mentioned the benefits that the rich were receiving from the labor of the lower classes, while lines 21–24 advise that no one should gain from this labor except the workers themselves. Therefore, for Question 6, the correct answer is B.

7.  The word "glance" in line 28 is closest in meaning to

    A.  skim
    B.  allude
    C.  strike
    D.  shine
    E.  glimpse

Question 7 falls in the "vocabulary" category of items. Notice, though, that the word "glance" is not a difficult word, not nearly as difficult as, say, "sesquipedalian." You see, usually when the exam asks you a question about an individual word, the way that you distinguish between multiple definitions for that word is more important than how well you have memorized a list of vocabulary. So, the set has built a question around "glance" to see how well you can determine its meaning in context.

Normally, the word "glance" relates to a quick look; that's why answers A and E have been included. But only the careless reader would choose one of these definitions, since they do not fit the context of the stanza. Nor does the word "allude" in B. C is an attractive distracter because the "tempered" steel that is doing the glancing might be used to strike a worker. However, in the stanza, the laborers themselves are just shaking their chains, so there is no striking or hitting going on here. D works best because, while the chains shake, reflected light (the sun pouring through a cell?) could glimmer on the laborers; in a metaphorical sense, the speaker is trying to get a new idea to "enlighten" the workers: that their toil is being treated unjustly by the upper classes.

If nothing else, the preposition "on" that follows "glance" is another hint that D is correct. From an idiomatic standpoint, something would not "skim on" you, "allude on" you, "strike on" you, or "glimpse on" you. But something could "shine on" you.

8.   The image in lines 27–28 implies that

    A.   the workers are responsible for their own subjugation

    B.   the craftsmanship of the workers is highly prized

    C.   a rebellion is close at hand

    D.   the oppression of the workers has lasted for centuries

    E.   the workers will be imprisoned if they strike

Even though Question 7 seems pretty isolated because it focuses only on one word, we now see that that the item is leading in to a more complex query in Question 8. Again, we would stress that as the questions proceed through the passage, their aim is to build meaning, to increase your understanding of the work.

If we understand that "glance" means "shine," our next step is to figure out why Shelley would envision the chains shining on the working men of England. In line 25, the speaker commands the workers to head for places underground, including "cells." Therefore, the chains must be those of a prison, probably a dungeon, into which only a little light would shine. Then, the speaker rhetorically asks why the workers would bother shaking the chains that they themselves have made. The implication is that the workers are enchained, that they wish to be free, but that, ironically, they cannot rid themselves of their own manacles. While the wealthy classes "dwell" in the decorated "halls" above (line 26), the workers inhabit the lower spaces willingly, because they have forged the instruments of their imprisonment. This image of confinement suggests that as long as they continue to labor without the proper recognition from those higher in society, the working classes will never be free in any sense. What "glances" off the steel and on the workers is not the light of pride (see B) or of hope (see C), but the light of awareness; the speaker wants them to know that they are allowing themselves to be treated unjustly. E cannot work because the workers are discussed in the stanza as if they are already in prison. The speaker never indicates in the poem how long the subjugation of the workers has lasted, so we do not have enough information to say that D is correct, either. Thus, the correct answer is A.

9.   The tone of the last stanza is

   A.   hopeful
   B.   indifferent
   C.   altruistic
   D.   sardonic
   E.   loathing

The term "tone" is one that you will see repeatedly on the AP Literature Exam in both the multiple-choice and essay sections. Remember that tone pertains to the attitude of the speaker, what he is feeling in a particular sentence, paragraph, or stanza, or in the passage as a whole.

At first, a careless reader might interpret the last stanza as having a hopeful tone. In lines 29–30, the workers seem independent. The upper classes are nowhere to be seen as the workers use instruments like plow, spade, and hoe to create burial spaces, and a loom to weave shrouds for themselves. In the end, laborers will be entombed in the earth of England, which the speaker calls "fair" or beautiful. So why couldn't we see the last stanza as a kind of positive closure?

The answer is that hope, at this point, would make no sense in the context of the whole poem. Despite his call to independence in lines 21–24, the speaker later sees the workers as willingly imprisoned (lines 25–28). He therefore implies that England's lower classes will not rally to save themselves from the tyranny of the rich. The last stanza, then, points to the only action that the workers can take for their own benefit: the preparation of their graves. Since no heavenly afterlife is mentioned here, how "fair" can England be when life for the country's poor has been one of oppression? Surely, then, the speaker sounds sardonic or scornful, D, mocking the workers who will not champion themselves and sneering at the country that keeps them down.

10. The slant rhyme of the last two lines ("fair/sepulchre") most likely reflects

    A. an imbalance of social justice
    B. the speaker's uncertainty
    C. the beauty of the workers' sacrifice
    D. the upper classes' realization of their wrongdoing
    E. a new change in the economic conditions of England

Here we have another "literary term" question. Anyone who takes the AP Literature Exam should have accumulated a large enough bank of literature-related terminology to answer these kinds of items correctly. For example, just as you had to know what "tone" was in Question 9, so, too, you are expected to understand the definition of "slant rhyme," which, as indicated by the words "fair" and "sepulchre," is a kind of near-rhyme, suggesting a lack of harmony.

For this reason, answers C, D, and E would not be suitable responses because they all connote a positive idea: the recognition of beauty or the restoration of order. B could be reflected in the inexactness of the slant rhyme, except that the speaker sounds so certain of himself throughout the poem that he even gives commands to the workers (lines 21–25). Only A matches the inharmonious sounds of "fair" and "sepulchre" with another kind of inequality: a lack of justice for the working men of England.

11. The "winding-sheet" (line 31) most suitably contrasts with

    A. "rich robes" (line 4)
    B. "Many a weapon, chain, and scourge" (line 10)
    C. "love's gentle balm" (line 14)
    D. "The arms ye forge" (line 20)
    E. "plough and spade and hoe and loom" (line 29)

No part of the passage is off limits to questions; even the footnotes are fair game. Therefore, don't ignore the footnotes when you read the passage.

In this case, when you see that a winding-sheet wraps around a corpse—that it is a kind of final clothing for a dead person—you can start to make some associations that prove A the right answer. Both a winding-sheet and rich robes are worn, but in the context of the poem there are two contrasting features about these garments. The winding-sheet is associated with the dead and is woven by the working class, while the rich robes are worn by those who are alive and wealthy. This opposition points out the inequity between the rich and the poor.

12.  The poem develops using all of the following EXCEPT

    A.   rhetorical questions
    B.   repetition
    C.   clothing imagery
    D.   similes
    E.   parallelism

We end the set with another item focusing on terms. Also notice that the final question asks you to reexamine the entire poem (as most final questions will). However, if you have been paying attention to the set, then the broad focus of Question 12 will not seem overwhelming.

For instance, Question 5 deals with the fourth and fifth stanzas, which feature rhetorical questions (A) and parallel structure (E). A quick scan of the poem reveals several more rhetorical questions, so B is now recognizable in the passage. Finally, we can see C in Question 11. Thus, even though similes are fairly common in poetry, they are not visible in this work, and D is the right answer.

## Strategy 4: Check the Stem's Boundaries

Besides trying to teach the passage to you, the questions of a multiple-choice set use other means to help you succeed as a critical reader. Take, for example, the careful phrasing of the stem, the part of the question appearing right before the answers. If you pay attention to the way that line numbers are brought up in the question, you'll know how big a chunk of the passage you can use to find your answer. Let's consider a set of questions about the Renaissance passage below. This time, we will concern ourselves with the way that the questions' stems control where you can look for evidence to make the right answer choice. (By the way, this example appears for the purpose of demonstration only; you will almost never find a piece of nonfiction on the AP Literature Exam).

*[In the following speech, Queen Elizabeth I is addressing her troops at Tillbury as they are about to defend England from attack.]*

My loving people, we have been persuaded by
some, that are careful of our safety, to take heed
how we commit ourselves to armed multitudes,
for fear of treachery; but I assure you, I do not
5    desire to live to distrust my faithful and loving
people. Let tyrants fear; I have always so behaved
myself that, under God, I have placed my chiefest strength and safeguard in the loyal hearts and
good will of my subjects. And therefore, I am
10   come amongst you at this time, not as for my recreation or sport, but being resolved, in the midst
and heat of the battle, to live or die amongst you
all; to lay down, for my God, and for my kingdom, and for my people, my honor and my blood,
15   even the dust. I know I have but the body of a
weak and feeble woman; but I have the heart of
a king, and of a king of England, too; and think
foul scorn that Parma[1] or Spain, or any prince
of Europe, should dare to invade the borders of
20   my realms: to which, rather than any dishonor

---

1    *Parma*: the duke of Parma, in Italy, who at the time of this speech was preparing
to invade England under the King of Spain's command.

should grow by me, I myself will take up arms,
I myself will be your general, judge, and rewarder
of every one of your virtues in the field. I know
already, by your forwardness, that you have
25   deserved rewards and crowns; and we do assure
you, on the word of a prince, they shall be duly paid
you. In the mean my lieutenant general shall be in
my stead, than whom never prince commanded
a more noble and worthy subject; not doubting
30   by your obedience to my general, by your con-
cord in the camp, and by your valor in the field,
we shall shortly have a victory over the enemies
of my God, of my kingdom, and of my people.
(1588)

1.   The speech is characterized by

A.   scolding and rebuke
B.   self-praise and egotism
C.   reassurance and encouragement
D.   inquiry and puzzlement
E.   pessimism and gloom

The stem refers to "The speech," so you have a wide set of boundaries here. You must consider the entire passage when determining the correct answer (C).

2.   The "armed multitudes" (line 3) of which the queen speaks are

A.   the English soldiers whom she is addressing
B.   the invading forces of Parma
C.   the people of England
D.   the "some" (line 21) who have given her recent advice
E.   the rulers of Europe

The parenthetical marker tells you that you can find the phrase "armed multitudes" in line 3, but you are not restricted to that line to determine your response. In fact, if you place the phrase in the context of the entire sentence in lines 1–6, you see that Queen Elizabeth makes a connection between the soldiers and her "loving people"; she thus is addressing her people, who also happen to be armed soldiers. The correct answer is A.

3.  The sentence in lines 6–9 ("Let tyrants fear...of my subjects.") attempts all of the following EXCEPT

    A.  to deny any tyranny on the part of the queen
    B.  to emphasize the queen's bravery in the upcoming battle against Spain
    C.  to hint that the queen may become a tyrant if the troops fail their mission
    D.  to underline the queen's regard for her people
    E.  to convince the audience of the queen's consistent behavior

Look at the way Question 3 is phrased compared to Question 2. This difference is important in comprehending how far you can go in the text to find your answer.

Unlike the previous item, Question 3 *does* restrict your movement in the text. The stem tells you that you only need to consider one sentence when deciding your answer. To move beyond this sentence would muddy your understanding of the question. So stay put when the stem tells you to! The correct answer here is C.

4.  Elizabeth refers to "recreation or sport" (lines 10–11) primarily to

    A.  show that she would abandon her leisure activities to support her troops
    B.  compare battle to a kind of dangerous game
    C.  imply that victory over Spain will be easily achieved
    D.  accuse her troops of taking their duties too lightly
    E.  demonstrate how serious she is in her purpose

Again, as in Question 2, the stem explains where a phrase is located, but does not bind you to that particular line. You'd be better off thinking of the phrase as part of a sentence to get an accurate read on its meaning. (The correct answer is E.)

5.  The phrase "even the dust" (line 15) shows

    A.  how willing Elizabeth is to lay down her life and pride

    B.  Elizabeth's need to "brush herself off" before she begins battle

    C.  that Elizabeth would sacrifice the very dust of her garments for England

    D.  Elizabeth's expectation that she will soon die in battle

    E.  that Elizabeth requires a level playing field when engaging the Spanish

The phrase being analyzed in Question 5 has an odd placement in the speech's third sentence, almost as if "even the dust" is an afterthought. However, the stem does not want you to think of the phrase in this kind of isolation. Once more, you are not restricted to a certain line when you make sense of "even the dust." In the entire third sentence, the phrase seems to be a part of this chain: "for my God, and for my kingdom, and for my people." Elizabeth would willingly die for these grander concepts, but then decides that she would part with her life even for the sake of England's dust. The correct answer is A.

6.  In lines 17–23, Elizabeth wants to "take up arms" (line 21) so that she can

    A.  right the previous injustices done to England

    B.  provide an example of proper field combat

    C.  seem more like a strong king than a weak queen

    D.  prove her power, patriotism, and bravery

    E.  filter out the cowards among her troops

Like Question 3, the stem here is forcing you to stay within the bounds of certain lines. The phrase "take up arms" is located for you in line 21, but the beginning of the stem tells you to expand your scope slightly to lines 17–23. Note that these lines are not a complete sentence. From time to time, a question set will have you look only at a segment of a sentence, or may ask you to examine a whole paragraph or stanza. At any rate, a key introduction to a stem will start with "In lines...." If you see this phrase, you know that you cannot exceed the provided line numbers. The correct answer is D.

7.   The sentence in lines 23–27 ("I know...paid you") implies that

   A.   Elizabeth will not pay the troops unless they defeat Spain
   B.   there is not enough money presently to pay the troops
   C.   honor and victory will be the only payment the troops receive
   D.   the troops feel they have not been paid what they are owed
   E.   a bonus will come to the troops if they remain loyal to the queen

   Some of the answers in Question 7 might be inferred from the passage as a whole, but you are confined to lines 23–27 only. Given this perimeter, you can only opt for D as a provable answer.

8.   The word "mean" in line 27 is closest in meaning to

   A.   average
   B.   cruel
   C.   indicate
   D.   meantime
   E.   meager

   By now, you should sense that this stem style frees you up to apply as much context as you need to select the right answer. However, you probably won't need to go beyond the sentence in which the quoted word appears. In fact, merely looking at the phrase "In the mean" (line 27) and plugging in the words above to replace "mean" ("In the average"; "In the cruel"; "In the indicate"; "In the meantime"; "In the meager") could give you the right answer (D) without too much work.

9.  All of the following are true about the "lieutenant general" (line 27)
    EXCEPT THAT

    A.  the queen thinks highly of him
    B.  he has commanded the troops before this time
    C.  he is being imbued with some of the queen's authority
    D.  the queen expects his orders to be followed
    E.  the queen anticipates the troops' harmonious behavior under
        his leadership

Question stems that lack clear line boundaries and end with the
phrase "EXCEPT THAT" tend to require you to look at more text
than usual. In this kind of situation, you have to prove four answers
correct and choose the one option that is false (B). Therefore, you
will probably have to explore more of the passage than with other
questions.

10. The passage develops mainly through the use of

    A.  contrast and parallelism
    B.  antithesis and rebuttal
    C.  analogy and metaphor
    D.  logical appeal and intellectualism
    E.  hearsay and rumor

As with the set's opening question, Question 10 asks you to review
the passage as a whole. No line should thus be ignored in answering this
question, but no line should be emphasized more than another, either.
Using this approach, you should notice that Queen Elizabeth often explains her motivations through (A), contrast ("I am not doing *this*; I am
doing *that*.") and parallel prepositional phrases ("for this, for this, for
this"; "of this, of this, of this.")

In every multiple-question, it is important to be aware of any limitations
the question stem sets on material involved. Think of the question stem as
a high fence that cordons off a backyard. Stay in your own backyard.

# Strategy 5: Context Controls Meaning

The implication of the previous strategy is that meaning is controlled by context. In different contexts, a sentence, a phrase, even a single word can change meaning. In the previous Queen Elizabeth set, for example, Question 8 asks about the word "mean." To answer correctly, you have to look at the sentence in which "mean" appears to determine what the word suggests.

To complicate matters, when you see the vocabulary questions in the multiple-choice section of the exam, you will notice that each of the possible answers tends to be a synonym for the word being asked about in the stem. Look how "mean" alters in each context implied by Question 8's answers:

A. The *mean* of 24, 86, and 103 is 71.

B. When you tease your sister about her braces, you are being *mean*.

C. What does the professor *mean* when she says "cogito ergo sum"?

D. Lassie fetched the farmers to save Timmy, who had fallen down the well. In the *mean*, Timmy's mother was home, unaware of her son's predicament.

E. Edgar sat at his dining room table and faced a *mean* supper: a dry biscuit and the last of the cabbage soup.

You can't rely on your expectations of a word's meaning to help you get the right answer in these situations. Only your analysis of context will carry you through.

But what if you have to understand not just a word, but an entire sentence? Since a sentence is a complete idea, doesn't it provide enough context on its own for you to comprehend it? The answer is "not necessarily, impetuous one." Look at the mock passage and question below:

"I'm giving you a choice, Desmond," Irene said softly, tears in her eyes. "You can take my hand. You can leave this dark room in your

mother's basement, and let her stop caring for you, her 34-year-old son.
You can finally be responsible for yourself. And you can love me, Des-
5  mond, as I love you." Desmond's throat felt hot and tight. "Or you can
turn your back to me, and continue to have your mother iron your un-
derwear and cut off the bread crusts of your baloney sandwiches." He
stood there, mouth open, stomach fluttering. Irene's hand, her lovely,
delicate hand, was held out for him. All he had to do was clasp it and the
10  whole, scary universe would be his. But his life was automatic, and he
liked it that way. Safely, he spun around to look at his bed, to take in the
aluminum bookshelves that housed his action figure collection and his
snow globes. He looked up at his sun, the bare, 70-watt bulb that hung
from the plywood ceiling, the floor of his mother's house. He would
15  protect this domain and be protected by it. A shuddering gasp escaped
him. He turned again and saw a gloom uninterrupted by the sweetness
of Irene's presence. He had not heard her leave. Obviously, Desmond
had made the right choice.

1.  What is the tone of the narrator's statement, "Obviously, Desmond
    had made the right choice"?

    A.  mocking
    B.  admiring
    C.  awestruck
    D.  regretful
    E.  matter-of-fact

If you concentrate only on the sentence itself, you may be tempted to
answer E, because the statement about Desmond lacks any kind of em-
bellishment. However, if you isolate the sentence from the context, you
make an uninformed decision about the implications of the sentence. The
question does not restrict you to a certain amount of lines in your analysis;
you are thus free to peruse the passage more widely to get your answer.

Then, if you consider the way that the passage presents Desmond's
pathetic life, and compare his need for security with the opportunity

that Irene is trying to give him, A becomes much more fitting. There is one more idea to note here. On rare occasions, students recognize a passage being examined in the multiple-choice section of the test. They may have seen the poem or prose excerpt in class, or could have read it on their own. Whatever the case, these students think that their additional knowledge will therefore help them answer the questions more accurately. However, such a notion is often mistaken. The AP multiple-choice items restrict themselves solely to the passage at hand. If you consider the passage in a context outside what the test gives you, you will wind up answering the questions incorrectly. If, for instance, a character in a passage is behaving in a heroic manner, but you know that, toward the end of the novel in which the character appears, he becomes villainous, you should not regard this change in answering the test questions. The final contextual restriction that you must keep in mind is the boundary of the test itself.

## Strategy 6: Not All Opinions are Equal

We often hear the word "opinion" used in the discussion of literature. Yet one opinion is not as good as the next. Some opinions are more insightful, more textually sound than others. And indeed some opinions are simply wrong. When discussing literature, then, you would be wise to think in terms not only of "right" and "wrong," but also in terms of "better than." Look at the passage below from F. Scott Fitzgerald's *The Great Gatsby*. Nick Carraway, the next-door neighbor, is describing a typical party one would discover on Gatsby's immense estate.

In the main hall a bar with a real brass rail was set up, and stocked with gins and liquors and with cordials so long forgotten that most of his female guests were too young to know one from another.

By seven o'clock the orchestra has arrived—no thin five piece affair
5   but a whole pit of oboes and trombones and saxophones and viols and cornets and piccolos and low and high drums. The last swimmers have

come in from the beach now and are dressing upstairs; the cars from New York are parked five deep in the drive, and already the halls and salons and verandas are gaudy with primary colors and hair shorn in
10  strange new ways and shawls beyond the dreams of Castile. The bar is in full swing and floating rounds of cocktails permeate the garden outside until the air is alive with chatter and laughter and casual innuendo and introductions forgotten on the spot and enthusiastic meetings between women who never knew each other's names.

One of the first questions to appear in the set for this passage goes like this:

2.   Between lines 3 and 4 there is a shift in verb tense which

   A.   indicates that Gatsby is a generous host
   B.   proves that Nick is feeling drunk
   C.   shows that Nick is an unconventional sort of man
   D.   causes the reader to question the reality of the party
   E.   makes the party sound more immediate

Now according to the reasoning, "Analyzing literature is just a matter of opinion," one could support all five answers above with the following opinions:

A. Gatsby *is* generous because his party is so lavish: lots of alcohol, a big band…people even have the freedom to change clothes in his house.

B. Since alcohol is being served at the party, Nick could be feeling drunk.

C. Most narrators tell their stories in past tense. Switching from past to present shows that Nick is an unusual kind of person.

D. Moving from past to present tense is a kind of time shift. Perhaps in being inconsistent with time, the reader can interpret that the party never existed at all.

E. The word "immediate" suggests "now." Present tense is occurring "now," so the verb tense shift makes the party seem as if it is not taking place in the past but in this moment.

However, as we said before, not all opinions have equal weight. Those which seem most textually relevant will win out in the end. Let us now rank the answers from least supportable to most:

D. Beware of answers that mention the reader. If we place our focus on reader reaction, we are pulling the question out of the text. Yet the only thing that the test wants to question is the text. Think about it: how can we say for sure what the reader is doing, when no two readers are alike? The text will remain unchanging, so we can ask questions about it and obtain consistent answers.

B. Nick discusses in the passage what he sees other people doing, not what he himself does. Alcohol flows freely at Gatsby's party, but Nick is not necessarily partaking. Furthermore, since he begins the description in past tense, we can make a reasonable assumption that the party has already taken place and that Nick is recalling what happened. The present tense shift is simply an effect he is adding to his storytelling.

C. Like B, C puts the emphasis on the state of the narrator, but Nick is not focusing on himself in this passage; rather, he is emphasizing the people and events of the party. Would it not be more logical to assume, therefore, that it is not the narrator who is unconventional, but the party? The rarity of the alcohol and the size of the band would certainly indicate so.

A. The text supports the idea that Gatsby is generous. What we must now do is make an association between generosity and present tense. What does one have to do with the other? What about past tense would preclude or even diminish the concept of being generous? The connection here seems weak.

E. The support for this answer appears logical and simple. No assumptions are made about *why* Nick would want to be more immediate in his description, only that he *is* more immediate.

Now, let's continue. That naive student might say, "When a multiple-choice question asks me something about a passage, I might see two or three answers that could be right. The test can't say I am wrong if I choose an answer that is right, but isn't necessarily the one they want me to choose."

Review those answers from the Gatsby question again. There is a way to view each of those answers so that they all sound feasible, to make two or three or even all five of them possible. But as we went back through and ranked them, we saw that the more we moved away from the text, the less likely the answer was. D was the worst because it had the least to do with Nick's description. A was what we might call an *attractive distracter*, because it was aligned with the way the passage presented Gatsby's festivities, but still made an illogical connection. The bottom line here is that two or three answers may seem right, but they do not all connect with the text equally.

Finally, our jaded student might say, "The whole test is designed to trick me, and I don't think it's fair." To view the test as a teasing bully gives a student permission to make himself less responsible as a thinker. If the fault is not in his reasoning skills, but in the attitude of the test, he cannot be blamed for doing poorly. What we are trying to suggest, however, is that a closer examination of the answers' phrasing and focus will make you a more discerning reader, and will lead to greater success with the AP Literature Exam. For this reason, you should look at *all* the answers before you select one as correct. If A sounds right, you should still consider B through E just in case one of them works better than A.

# Essay Writing Strategies

Doing well on the essay portion of the exam takes skill, practice, and of course a good strategy. In the following pages, we will work through the strategies that will help you maximize your score on this portion of the exam.

## Strategy 1: Manage Your Time

You have two hours for the essay portion of the exam. Since there are three essays to write, you have an average of forty minutes to write each essay. However, you may not want to give the same amount of time to each writing task; one may seem more difficult than the other two, or another may seem ridiculously easy to you. Don't feel obligated to give each essay the full forty minutes. On the other hand, don't waste time. If you finish all three essays in less than two hours, go back and review your responses. You will undoubtedly find some error that needs correction or some point that requires further explanation.

## Strategy 2: Prioritize

Before you start writing, look at all three prompts and the passages that accompany them, so that you face no surprises deep into your essay writing. The first essay always deals with a poem, sometimes two. The second essay deals with a prose passage, usually taken from a short story or novel, sometimes even a play. Both the poem and prose prompts are broad and brief. The last essay asks you to apply a general question to a major work you have read. This last prompt is referred to as the "open question." Once you have read over all three essay prompts, you need to decide on a strategy for writing them. Take a minute and think about which essay of the three you would find easiest to write, and which you would find most challenging. Because you have only two hours to write all three, you must ask yourself, which do you want to write first? Here are two approaches to this question:

**Approach 1:** One school of thought says that you should write the most difficult essay first and save the easiest for last. The benefits of this approach are twofold: a) if you get crunched for time at the end of the writing session, you will be more comfortable dealing with your strongest topic, and b) you will have something to look forward to at the end of the testing period.

**Approach 2:** Another line of thinking is that you should write the least difficult essay first and save the hard one for last. That way, you begin your writing by being more at ease, and if you are losing time at the end of the test…well, the most difficult essay wasn't going to be your best one, anyway, so if you only have 20 minutes left to write it, it's not such a loss. At least you made a strong showing with the first two essays you wrote.

What we do *not* recommend is that you dive right into the first essay, the poetry response, without even looking at the other two beforehand, and then simply proceed chronologically through the questions. Writers who take this approach tend to be less engaged by the test and are merely trying to get it over with. Their essays more than likely will have a mundane, uninspired quality to them.

# Strategy 3: Plan Your Essay

Let's say on test day, you look at the student next to you and she is opening her test booklet. She reads the first essay prompt. And...she starts to write. What happened to her pre-planning steps? Does she honestly think that her mind is organized enough to keep her thoughts orderly on the page without taking a few notes first?

It may seem that your fellow student has a head start in her writing, but in reality she has handicapped herself. You will end up with a better, higher-scoring essay if you plan your response. One way is to use the AEIOU Method:

A is for ANNOTATE: Mark up the text. Write marginal notes. Do not be cautious. Write whatever comes to mind. Even if the thoughts that are popping up seem silly, write them down anyway. You never know what you may be able to use.

E. is for ENGAGE: Engage the text in two ways. First, engage with the essay prompt. Be certain of its requirements, restrictions, and implications. Use these as a frame for engaging with the passage. Then, as you read the passage, or the list of works in the open question, allow yourself to become involved in what is happening. Let the passage entertain, inform, or persuade you. (Just because it's in a test doesn't mean it's boring. Some very smart people put it in the test because they thought it had some kind of engaging quality about it.) As you read the list of works in the third question, think about the ones you've read. Which ones afforded you the most pleasure? Which ones changed the way you thought about the world? Wouldn't it be more pleasant to write about the one that you had the best relationship with?

"I" is for INTERCONNECT: Chances are good that one reason the poetic and prose passages were chosen for your test is that they were rich, unified texts. Therefore, you cannot simply annotate these passages; you must also see the patterns and connections within them. As you engage with the passage and write notes in its margins, you should also indicate with arrows and arcing lines where you see similarities, repetitions, configurations of opposites, etc. Is it really a coincidence, for instance, that the main character uses several images of darkness when she is being asked advice about relationships? What would such a pattern imply? Understanding the interconnectedness of the text will lead you to discover its larger themes.

"O" is for OUTLINE: We have said so earlier in this guide, but it bears repeating: if you take time to outline what you will write in your essay, you will actually be saving yourself some time on the test.

An outline can indicate to you what the best organizational strategy will be for your writing; in the open question, an outline may warn you away from choosing *The Scarlet Letter* as your text of choice and lead you to selecting *Fahrenheit 451* instead. If you don't write the outline ahead of time, then halfway through your *Scarlet Letter* response, you could realize, "Oh, no. This isn't going to work. I just hit a dead end." Then you either have to start over (tick-tock, tick-tock) or you have to force your chosen work to fit the question when you know it doesn't, really. Our thoughts are not characteristically well-ordered. Outlining can make them so.

"U" is for UNDERLINE: The most basic, rudimentary way to make sense of your text is to underline certain aspects of it. Underlining creates emphasis, erects sign posts so that you can return later and include in your essay what you previously marked in the passage.

However, underlining is not enough. If people are going to make marks on a text while they read, most of them will only underline. The problem is that if they stop there, then when they go back through the text they can forget the reason why they underlined something in the first place. Therefore, underlining should only take place if it is accompanied by annotation.

Ready to see the AEIOU method in action? Of course you are. We'll begin with some ordinary UNDERLINING.

Read the following poem carefully. Then, write a well-organized essay in which you explain how the poem <u>encourages an appreciation of nature</u>. You may include—but are not restricted to—<u>imagery, sound devices, narrative shifts, and parallelism</u>.

### The Fish, the Man and the Spirit

*To a Fish*
You strange, astonished-looking, <u>angle-faced</u>,
Dreary-mouthed, gaping wretches of the sea,
Gulping salt-water everlastingly,
Cold-blooded, though with red your blood be graced,

5   And mute, though dwellers in the <u>roaring waste</u>;
And you, all shapes beside, that fishy be—
Some round, some flat, some long, all <u>devilry</u>,
Legless, unloving, <u>infamously chaste</u>—

O scaly, slippery wet, swift, staring wights[1],
10  <u>What is't ye do? What life lead?</u> Eh, dull goggles?
How do ye vary your vile days and nights?
How pass your Sundays? Are ye still but joggles
In ceaseless wash? Still nought but <u>gapes, and bites,</u>
<u>And drinks, and stares</u>, diversified with boggles[2]?

---

1    *wights:* creatures

2    *boggles:* sudden movements

*A Fish Answers*

15 Amazing monster! That, for aught I know,

With the first sight of thee didst make our race

Forever stare! Oh flat and shocking face,

Grimly divided from the breast below!

Thou that on dry land horribly dost go

20 With a split body and ridiculous pace,

Prong after prong, disgracer of all grace,

Long-useless-finned, haired upright, unwet, slow!


O breather of unbreathable, sword-sharp air,

How canst exist? How bear thyself, thou dry

25 And dreary sloth? What particle canst share

Of the only blessed life, the watery?

I sometimes see of ye an actual pair

Go by! Linked fin by fin! odiously.


*The Fish Turns Into a Man, and Then Into a Spirit, and Again Speaks*

Indulge thy smiling scorn, if smiling still,

30 O man! And loathe, but with a sort of love;

For difference must its use by difference prove,

And in such sweet clang, the spheres with music fill.

One of the spirits am I, that at his will

Live in whate'er has life—fish, eagle, dove—

35 No hate, no pride, beneath nought, nor above,

A visitor of the rounds of God's sweet skill.


Man's life is warm, glad, sad, 'twixt loves and graves,

Boundless in hope, honored with pangs austere,

Heaven-gazing; and his angel-wings he craves:

40 The fish is swift, small-needing, vague yet clear,

A cold, sweet, silver life, wrapped in round waves,

Quickened with touches of transporting fear.

(1836)

Again, underlining is not enough. It does not provide enough explanation in its note taking. Let's now add the steps of ENGAGING the prompt and ANNOTATING the text. The margin notes correspond to the underlining near them:

Read the following poem very carefully. Then, write a well-organized essay in which you explain how the <u>poem encourages an appreciation of nature</u>. You may include—but are not restricted to—<u>imagery, sound devices, narrative shifts, and parallelism</u>.

*Nature is
a good thing
in poem.*

## The Fish, the Man and the Spirit

### To a Fish

You strange, astonished-looking, <u>angle-faced</u>,

Dreary-mouthed, gaping wretches of the sea,          *lacks*

Gulping salt-water everlastingly,                    *human*

Cold-blooded, though with red your blood be graced,  *quality*

5  And mute, though dwellers in the <u>roaring waste</u>;

And you, all shapes beside, that fishy be—

Some round, some flat, some long, all <u>devilry</u>,

Legless, unloving, <u>infamously chaste</u>—

*Not just subhu—
man but demonic*

*hy is this
ad? how is* 10 <u>O scaly, slippery wet, swift, staring wights,</u>

*his*        <u>What is't ye do? What life lead?</u> Eh, dull goggles?  *lack of purpose*

*ssible?*    How do ye vary your vile days and nights?        *bothers speaker*

How pass your Sundays? Are ye still but joggles

In ceaseless wash? Still nought but <u>gapes, and bites,</u>

<u>And drinks, and stares</u>, diversified with boggles?

### A Fish Answers

15  Amazing monster! That, for aught I know,

<u>With the first sight of thee didst make our race</u>      *synecdoche*

<u>Forever stare</u>! Oh flat and shocking face,

Grimly divided from the breast below!

Thou that on dry land horribly dost go

20 With a split body and ridiculous pace,

*throwing it back in human's face*

Prong after prong, disgracer of all grace,

Long-useless-finned, haired upright, <u>unwet</u>, slow!

*Characterized by what we are not*

O breather of <u>unbreathable</u>, sword-sharp air,

How canst exist? How bear thyself, thou dry

25 And dreary sloth? What particle canst share

Of the only blessed life, the watery?

I sometimes see of ye <u>an actual pair</u>

<u>Go by! Linked fin by fin! odiously.</u>

*Even our fellowship is odd*

### The Fish Turns Into a Man, and Then Into a Spirit, and Again Speaks

Indulge thy smiling scorn, if smiling still,

30 O man! And <u>loathe, but with a sort of love</u>;

<u>For difference must its use by difference prove</u>,

And in such <u>sweet clang</u>, the spheres with music fill.

One of the spirits am I, that at his will

Live in whate'er has life—fish, eagle, dove—

35 No hate, no pride, beneath nought, nor above,

A visitor of the rounds of God's sweet skill.

*antithesis and parallel structure indicate harmonious discovery by fish spirit*

<u>Man 's life is warm, glad, sad, 'twixt loves and graves</u>,

<u>Boundless in hope, honored with pangs austere</u>,

<u>Heaven-gazing; and his angel-wings he craves</u>:

40 The fish is swift, small-needing, vague yet clear,

A cold, sweet, silver life, wrapped in round waves,

Quickened with touches of <u>transporting fear</u>.

*we both have our own beauty and motivation*

(1836)

Now, imagine that the annotations are still there, but we are next going to include marks that suggest INTERCONNECTIONS in the text:

## The Fish, the Man and the Spirit

*To a Fish*

You strange, astonished-looking, angle-faced,

Dreary-mouthed, gaping wretches of the sea,

Gulping salt-water everlastingly,

Cold-blooded, though with red your blood be graced,

5    And mute, though dwellers in the roaring waste;

And you, all shapes beside, that fishy be—

Some round, some flat, some long, all devilry,

Legless, unloving, infamously chaste—

O scaly, slippery wet, swift, staring wights,

10    What is't ye do? What life lead? Eh, dull goggles?

How do ye vary your vile days and nights?

How pass your Sundays? Are ye still but joggles

In ceaseless wash? Still nought but gapes, and bites,

And drinks, and stares, diversified with boggles?

*A Fish Answers*

15    Amazing monster! That, for aught I know,

With the first sight of thee didst make our race

Forever stare! Oh flat and shocking face,

Grimly divided from the breast below!

Thou that on dry land horribly dost go

20    With a split body and ridiculous pace,

Prong after prong, disgracer of all grace,

Long-useless-finned, haired upright, unwet, slow!

O breather of unbreathable, sword-sharp air,

How canst exist? How bear thyself, thou dry

25    And dreary sloth? What particle canst share

Of the only blessed life, the watery?

"astonished-looking,"
"angle-faced" why
alliterate?

"O scaly," "O breather"
addressed in same way

I sometimes see of ye <u>an actual pair</u>
<u>Go by! Linked fin by fin!</u> odiously.

### The Fish Turns Into a Man, and Then Into a Spirit, and Again Speaks

Indulge thy smiling scorn, if smiling still,

30 O man! And <u>loathe, but with a sort of love;</u>
   <u>For difference must its use by difference prove,</u>
   And in such <u>sweet clang</u>, the spheres with music fill.
   One of the spirits am I, that at his will
   Live in whate'er has life—fish, eagle, dove—

35 No hate, no pride, beneath nought, nor above,
   A visitor of the rounds of God's sweet skill.

   <u>Man 's life is warm, glad, sad, 'twixt loves and graves,</u>
   <u>Boundless in hope, honored with pangs austere,</u>
   <u>Heaven-gazing; and his angel-wings he craves:</u>

40 The fish is swift, small-needing, vague yet clear,
   A cold, sweet, silver life, wrapped in round waves,
   Quickened with touches of <u>transporting fear.</u>

opposites: hope and fear

(1836)

Finally, we can transform all of this note-taking into an outline that will guide the organization of our first essay:

<u>Fish essay</u>

  I. Differences cause repulsion

 II. Human to fish

     A. images of inhuman appearance

     B. lack of purpose

     C. finalized with synecdoche that minimizes fish's significance

III. Parallel structure shows fish hate humans

     A. "O scaly...wights" vs. "O breather"

     B. Disliking what is unlike itself

IV. Fish becomes spirit and reveals truth of man's/fish's beauty

    A. Why does the fish change and not the man?

    B. What do differences uncover?

    C. Instead of being repulsed by differences, why we should appreciate them?

Notice that not all your annotations and interconnections made the final cut in your outline. There is no need to include every single note you made. Some should be discarded because they will not fit into your thesis.

Give yourself about ten minutes to go through this AEIOU method for pre-planning your essay. You will then have a solid half hour of actual essay writing, but a half hour in which you can feel more confident because you know exactly what you want to say.

## Strategy 4: A Well-Balanced Introduction

Let's image once again that you are at the test site. As you sit at your desk getting ready to write the second essay—on the prose passage—five other students nervously contemplate how they will write their introductions. Somehow, you have developed telepathy and can "hear" each introduction as it is formulating in the heads of these five students. You then gather that the reason why you have just been blessed with this supernatural insight is that you are being taught how *not* to write an introduction. Lucky you!

Let's practice by examining the following prose passage:

In the following passage from Kate Chopin's short story, "A Pair of Silk Stockings," Mrs. Sommers has left her home to go shopping in the city for her children's new clothes. Discuss the way the passage develops characterization. You may include—but are not limited to—point of view, syntax, and symbolism.

She had seen some beautiful patterns, veritable bargains in the shop windows. And still there would be left enough for new stockings—two pairs apiece—and what darning that would save for a while! She would get caps for the boys and sailor hats for the girls. The vision of her little

5 brood looking fresh and dainty and new for once in their lives excited her and made her restless and wakeful with anticipation.

The neighbors sometimes talked of "better days" that little Mrs. Sommers had known before she had ever thought of being Mrs. Sommers. She herself indulged in no such morbid retrospection. She had no time—

10 no second of time to devote to the past. The needs of the present absorbed her every faculty. A vision of the future like some dim, gaunt monster sometimes appalled her, but luckily to-morrow never comes.

Mrs. Sommers was one who knew the value of bargains; who could stand for hours making her way inch by inch toward the desired object

15 that was selling below cost. She would elbow her way if need be; she had learned to clutch a piece of goods and hold it and stick to it with persistence and determination till her turn came to be served, no matter when it came.

But that day she was a little faint and a little tired. She had swallowed

20 a light luncheon—no! when she came to think of it, between getting the children fed and the place righted, and preparing herself for the shopping bout, she had actually forgotten to eat any luncheon at all!

She sat herself upon a revolving stool before a counter that was comparatively deserted, trying to gather strength and courage to charge

25 through an eager multitude that was besieging breastworks of shirting and figured lawn. An all-gone limp feeling had come over her and she rested her hand aimlessly upon the counter. She wore no gloves. By degrees she grew aware that her hand had encountered something very soothing, very pleasant to touch. She looked down to see that her hand

30 lay upon a pile of silk stockings. A placard near by announced that they had been reduced in price from two dollars and fifty cents to one dollar and ninety-eight cents; and a young girl who stood behind the counter asked her if she wished to examine their line of silk hosiery. She smiled,

just as if she had been asked to inspect a tiara of diamonds with the ul-
35 timate view of purchasing it. But she went on feeling the soft, sheeny
luxurious things—with both hands now, holding them up to see them
glisten, and to feel them glide serpent-like through her fingers.

Two hectic blotches came suddenly into her pale cheeks. She looked
up at the girl.

40 "Do you think there are any eights-and-a-half among these?"


Now, let's listen in as your fellow test takers think up absolutely
horrific introductions for their responses, introductions that any self-
respecting English teacher would slash to tatters and bury in a cornfield
at midnight.


## Agnes, the Generalizer

*Throughout history, women have shopped for their children's clothes. The
earliest cave dwellers probably made their own clothes out of animal skins
and sold them to each other for bones and rocks, while today's mothers go
to the mall or even buy garments online from The Gap. Mrs. Sommers,
in Chopin's "A Pair of Silk Stockings," is no exception. The passage opens
with her actually being excited at the thought of purchasing clothing for her
"brood"; however, by the end of the passage, Mrs. Sommers has turned her
focus on herself and has completely forgotten the needs of her children. Those
cave dwellers would certainly be ashamed of this transformation.*

Agnes has started *so broadly* that she is going far beyond the passage
and attempting to include *all of human history* in her scope. Just how
adequately can one talk about *all of human history* in one paragraph?
Because of Agnes' awkwardly epic scope, she winds up shifting her
thesis back to the cave dwellers instead of Mrs. Sommers. Such an approach is unhelpful. The introduction—indeed, the entire essay—should
stay focused on Mrs. Sommers' characterization. We don't need mention of cave people, the Gap, or online shopping. Talk generally about

Mrs. Sommers' situation, then narrow down to the point you want to make about her character.

### Fred, the Throat Clearer

*A woman enters a department store. She is tired. She is thinking about all the domestic responsibilities weighing her down. There is her little boy Johnny at home, with his toes protruding from his frayed stockings. Then there is Janey, the bright one, the optimistic one, who always has a kind word for Mother when she gets home, but secretly hides a small tear when Mother turns her back to resume her daily chores. Such are the burdens facing Mrs. Sommers in Chopin's "A Pair of Silk Stockings." As Mrs. Sommers ruminates on what clothing she will buy those little dear ones at home, she suddenly notices a pile of silk stockings under her ungloved hand. They transport her to scenes of masquerade balls, cool summer nights, kisses stolen under elm trees. This is what she has been missing since her hard years with Mr. Sommers: a little luxury, a chance to return to excess. The passage shows that Mrs. Sommers acts one way in the beginning and then an entirely different way by the end.*

Fred seems to have forgotten that he has 40 minutes to write this essay. He has become entirely lost in his introduction, which is more creative writing than analysis. In fact, so self-absorbed is Fred that he manufactures a meaningless backstory on Mrs. Sommers and ends the intro with a vague and futile thesis. He is just clearing his throat, or stalling, until some idea pops into his head.

### Cecil, the Dumper

*Kate Chopin, in her story "A Pair of Silk Stockings," portrays Mrs. Sommers as a dissatisfied housewife who finds out that she doesn't just have to shop for her kids; she can buy something for herself, too.*

Cecil, unlike Fred, seems acutely aware of his time limit. He wants to get to the body of his essay pronto, so he does not waste time on an elaborate introduction. He dumps in front of you the basic essentials and speeds to the next paragraph. The problem is that he has given us so little to work with in this single sentence that we cannot determine any significant idea about to rear its head in his essay. We admire his ability to remain in the text—Agnes and Fred did not—but we would like to see him infused a bit with Fred's talent for explication.

### Bertha, the Tape Recorder

*Mrs. Sommers is faced with a dilemma. She can buy clothes for her children, or she can purchase a pair of silk stockings for herself. Kate Chopin, in her short story, "A Pair of Silk Stockings," discusses Mrs. Sommers' characterization through point of view, syntax, and symbolism.*

Bertha is direct, much like Cecil, but she has a better sense of thesis development than he does. We know by the end of her introduction exactly what she plans to do: she'll discuss three elements in the passage that develop Mrs. Sommers as a character. Great. The problem is that Bertha is just repeating what she read in the prompt. We can't tell if she has any original ideas in her head or not. This is the kind of intro that hints at the following: as the essay's body proceeds, Bertha will name an element, quote part of the passage that contains that element, and mindlessly repeat that this quoted example shows Mrs. Sommers' character. There will be no explanation of the *way* in which point of view or symbolism reveals what is happening with Mrs. Sommers. Bertha is doomed to *mention*, to *list*, not to *explore*. On a 9-point scale, she is headed for a 5.

### Irving, the Flatterer

*In the classic tale "A Pair of Silk Stockings," told extremely well by Kate Chopin, Mrs. Sommers is a timeless character who is burdened by her life as a mother. Chopin does a great job of making us empathize with poor Mrs. Sommers, who can't catch a break in her tough life. This short masterpiece helps us realize that life is too short, and we should live it to the fullest.*

Like Fred, Irving obviously does not know what to analyze in the passage. Instead, he thinks that if he compliments the story and the author, we will reward his appreciation of fine art. Instead, he is demonstrating how empty his thoughts are. He is only ready to talk about the passage on a largely thematic, clichéd level. We are less interested in the lesson that the story wants to teach than in the elements the story uses to create meaning.

Unlike Agnes, Fred, Cecil, Bertha, and Irving, you know that your introduction must balance exposition and analysis. You have to refer to the events of the passage (or the content of the poem in the first question, or the plot of the major work in the third question) so that you can narrow down to a thesis that will explain how various aspects of the passage create unified meaning. However, you can't just repeat what you've seen in the prompt. So, you write something like the following:

*In Chopin's "A Pair of Silk Stockings," Mrs. Sommers is a woman in transition, and she is as unaware of the new decision she is about to make as she is of the stockings under her ungloved hand—at first. Her original intent in the department store is to buy clothes for her children, but as the "sheeny" fabric of the stockings begins to seduce her, her mind will empty itself of her domestic charges and begin to fill with silky luxury. Yet Chopin's omniscient narrator uses several techniques to ensure that Mrs. Sommers remains a sympathetic character, instead of a selfish woman who is heedless of her children's needs.*

In this example, you stayed in the text, unlike Agnes or Fred, and gave us only enough exposition to set up your analysis, unlike Irving, who had no analysis. You weren't overly brief, like Cecil, and you didn't merely repeat the prompt the way that Bertha did. Your announcement that the "omniscient narrator" makes Mrs. Sommers "sympathetic" is a clear reference to the prompt's suggestion that you examine "point of view" to reveal characterization, so we know that you aren't straying from the prompt.

# Strategy 5: Give Just Enough Direction

If you look at the "good" introduction paragraph from the previous example, you can see that it indicates where it is going, but it doesn't pound out every detail. There is a point when an introduction can overexplain itself, and in so doing, can sound mechanical, rehearsed, and amateurish. Consider this unfortunate alteration to the last part of the introduction:

*Yet Chopin's omniscient narrator uses background information, unreliability, and biblical allusion to ensure that Mrs. Sommers remains a sympathetic character, instead of a selfish woman who is heedless of her children's needs.*

One might argue that this thesis is more informative than the previous example. This is true, but by enumerating what the narrator does to make Mrs. Sommers likeable, we have new problems. First, in an attempt to attach labels to the narrator's techniques, the introduction now sounds more confusing. How does one define "background information"? What is "unreliability" and how can it be something that a narrator "uses"? And how can "biblical allusion" work in the same way as these other elements? Second, by listing exactly three methods employed by the narrator, you sound as if you are going to subject us to a formulaic five-paragraph essay, a handy tool for rookie writers, but not a recipe for a high-scoring essay. Third, by laying everything out in the beginning, you are preventing yourself from discovering something new as you write the essay. The modified introduction sounds as though it is on a set track and cannot find any alternative but appropriate destinations. How dull!

Therefore, your introduction should indicate where the essay is going, but shouldn't make the trip sound as if it has a foregone conclusion.

# Strategy 6: Choose Good Examples

We are now exiting the introduction and entering the body of the essay. Once you decide what element or elements you are going to discuss, you have to figure out what examples are best to use for your approach. The body of the essay must have examples that fit into three categories: appropriateness, variety, and originality. Once more, let's haul in the intro paragraph for the prose prompt:

*In Chopin's "A Pair of Silk Stockings," Mrs. Sommers is a woman in transition, and she is as unaware of the new decision she is about to make as she is of the stockings under her ungloved hand—at first. Her original intent in the department store is to buy clothes for her children, but as the "sheeny" fabric of the stockings begins to seduce her, her mind will empty itself of her domestic charges and begin to fill with silky luxury. Yet Chopin's omniscient narrator uses several techniques to ensure that Mrs. Sommers remains a sympathetic character, instead of a selfish woman who is heedless of her children's needs.*

The textual examples supporting this introduction must first be *appropriate*. All of the following excerpts from the Chopin passage demonstrate the narrator's omniscience referred to in the intro; however, one is more appropriate for your essay than the others:

a. "She had seen some beautiful patterns, veritable bargains in the shop windows."

b. "The neighbors sometimes talked of 'better days' that little Mrs. Sommers had known."

c. "Mrs. Sommers was one who knew the value of bargains."

d. "She smiled, just as if she had been asked to inspect a tiara of diamonds."

If we need to discuss, as the introduction says, not only the narrator's omniscience, but also the *way* in which the narrator creates sympathy for Mrs. Sommers, then b is the best choice for your essay. The narrator knows of people who understand Mrs. Sommers' current difficulties. One is less likely to fault her consideration of the stocking purchase if he knows that Mrs. Sommers has suffered a decline. A less skillful writer, however, may have referred to any of the quotes, simply because they demonstrated the narrator's omniscience.

The second characteristic that your body must have is *variety*. The more variable your examples, the more extensively they encompass your thesis. One way to create variety is to list widely differing aspects of the text that prove a thesis true. For example, Bertha repeated the prompt's suggestions for discussion: "Kate Chopin, in her short story, 'A Pair of Silk Stockings,' discusses Mrs. Sommers' characterization through point of view, syntax and symbolism." Bertha certainly does have variety here, but may run into a problem. If she only discusses one example of each element, and more importantly, does not relate these examples to one another, she will create a false sense of variety. If she can't connect her examples in meaningful ways, why did she bring them into discussion with each other in the first place?

A better way to create variety is by finding multiple examples of the same kind of element, and discovering subtle but significant differences between them. For instance, your good introduction only deals with the element of point of view. The danger in this approach is that your textual examples can too easily act in the same way. But if you can point out the unique differences among them, then you create variety where only similarity seemed to exist. Look at this set of examples:

a. "The neighbors sometimes talked of 'better days' that little Mrs. Sommers had known."

b. "She had no time—no second of time to devote to the past. The needs of the present absorbed her every faculty."

c. "She had swallowed a light luncheon—no! when she came to think of it, between getting the children fed and the place righted, and preparing herself for the shopping bout, she had actually forgotten to eat any luncheon at all!"

d. "But she went on feeling the soft, sheeny luxurious things—with both hands now, holding them up to see them glisten, and to feel them glide serpent-like through her fingers."

As before, each one is an example of the narrator's omniscience some-how creating sympathy for Mrs. Sommers, right? So they all are the same and have no variety, right? Wrong! Here is what you would point out about each one:

a. The neighbors can confirm that Mrs. Sommers' life is not as good as it used to be. Poor Mrs. Sommers!

b. Even though the neighbors note Mrs. Sommers' hardships, she doesn't feel sorry for herself. Brave Mrs. Sommers!

c. She is so busy taking care of her children's needs that she can actu-ally forget to take care of herself. Self-sacrificing Mrs. Sommers!

d. She sounds like Eve being tempted by the serpent in the Garden of Eden. Victimized Mrs. Sommers!

Each example proves the presence of a narrator who can know things that the casual observer does not, but each example sympathizes with Mrs. Sommers in a different way. There's the variety.

The last aspect that your examples need to have is *originality*. If you can find an innovative way to present your ideas, then you can make your essay stand out among the thousands that one AP reader may score. Another problem with Bertha's "point of view, syntax, and symbolism" approach is that so many students are going to be following in her foot-steps. Unable or unwilling to claim ownership of their own creativity, a large portion of students taking the AP Literature Exam are just going to let the question do the thinking for them. However, you can preserve your creativity by keeping in mind two factors:

1. If you take our advice on the best way to have variety in your re-sponse (multiple examples of a single element, like point of view), then in a sense you are already being more original than many writ-ers taking the exam.

2. Understand that even if the question tells you to consider elements like point of view, syntax, and symbolism, you are not restricted to

them. What if you went after the images of the monster in the second paragraph and the serpent in the last line? What is similar about them as a set? What is subtly different about them? What if you linked the articles of clothing together in the passage, not just the stockings, but the mention of caps, sailor hats, and gloves? What pattern brings them together? The elements in the prompt are just suggestions. Use them if you need to, but if you can find something on your own that is not only original but also appropriate and variable, you'll do well for yourself.

## Strategy 7: Organize Your Points Climactically

Yes, organization matters. Sometimes, following the order of the text is appropriate, but too often a chronological arrangement indicates an oversimplified and disconnected argument. Take, for instance, the textual examples from the Chopin passage:

a. "The neighbors sometimes talked of 'better days' that little Mrs. Sommers had known…"

b. "She had no time—no second of time to devote to the past. The needs of the present absorbed her every faculty."

c. "She had swallowed a light luncheon—no! when she came to think of it, between getting the children fed and the place righted, and preparing herself for the shopping bout, she had actually forgotten to eat any luncheon at all!"

d. "But she went on feeling the soft, sheeny luxurious things—with both hands now, holding them up to see them glisten, and to feel them glide serpent-like through her fingers."

If you built the body of your essay on these quotations and kept them in this arrangement because this is the order in which they appear in the text, you could write an effective essay. However, if you reconsider the order in which you discuss them, your essay may develop more unity and pizzazz. Try, for example, discussing the text sample that generates the least amount of sympathy for Mrs. Sommers and build your way up to the item that generates the most.

### "Least to Most Sympathy" Organization

a. "She had swallowed a light luncheon—no! when she came to think of it, between getting the children fed and the place righted, and preparing herself for the shopping bout, she had actually forgotten to eat any luncheon at all!"

If the body of the essay begins by analyzing this quotation, then you could say that Mrs. Sommers is obviously weak and hungry when she encounters the silk stockings. Her defenses are down, so she is more susceptible to temptation. However, you could also admit that her hunger is a temporary physical ailment and that there are more significant ways in which the narrator can portray Mrs. Sommers sympathetically. Next, you move to a discussion of the following excerpt.

b. "The neighbors sometimes talked of 'better days' that little Mrs. Sommers had known…"

We see here that Mrs. Sommers' life is not as good as it used to be. The addition of the word "little" also emphasizes how vulnerable she is to life's travails. This condition is more intense than mere hunger. The problem has been going on for some time, and may be more socially or financially based. By presenting this point second, you begin to ramp up the case for making Mrs. Sommers more blameless for giving in to the silk stockings.

c. "She had no time—no second of time to devote to the past. The needs of the present absorbed her every faculty."

This excerpt continues to paint Mrs. Sommers in a positive light because she is not feeling sorry for herself, despite her fall from "better days." We have to discuss quote b before we can understand c.

d. "But she went on feeling the soft, sheeny luxurious things—with both hands now, holding them up to see them glisten, and to feel them glide serpent-like through her fingers."

This quote takes on new significance in this configuration because, by now, we have explained why Mrs. Sommers almost deserves these stockings. The description of their texture and appearance makes them seem especially desirable, as if Mrs. Sommers—in her hungry, abject state—could not help but want to purchase them.

Another organizational approach may be to discuss quote d first and then "flash back" to a discussion of the other quotes.

### "Flashback" Organization

Using this method, a writer could look at Mrs. Sommers' encounter with the silk stockings out of context. If we explain that she is at the store to buy clothes for her children and then show her running the hosiery through her fingers, we start to depict her as an irresponsible parent. However, we can then go back to the "better days" quote and the rest of the evidence essentially to reexamine Mrs. Sommers' situation. Ultimately, by the time the last quote is discussed, we justify her desire for the stockings.

Of course, there are other organizations one could ponder, but the point we want to make is that if you save *the most important or least obvious example for last*, your essay ends with a bang; you sound more convincing.

## Strategy 8: Avoid Discussing the Reader

Remember Agnes the Generalizer and Irving the Flatterer? One of the things that made their introductions so hideous is that they placed their focus outside the text. This test that you are about to take is the Advanced Placement Literature exam, with a heavy emphasis on "Literature"; you shouldn't be discussing anything besides the text in your essay: not history, not empty praise for the author, not personal stories, not hypothetical situations…and you should never discuss the reader in your essay. Let's say you were given this prompt for the final essay:

In a well-developed essay, select one of the works below and explain the way that one of its characters gains new insight into his or her society simply by existing on the fringes of that society. Ultimately, what is the impact of this new perception on the individual's civilization?

Here is a part of one writer's essay, which uses the example of Hawthorne's *The Scarlet Letter*:

*Hawthorne causes the reader to pity Reverend Dimmesdale. As the Puritan minister stands on the scaffold, exposing the burning A on his chest to the heavens, we can't help but wonder how he can feel so tortured. The reader aches for him, and we want him to be able to walk up to Hester and say, "I love you. Will you marry me and let me be a father to little Pearl?" The reader can almost feel the letter A burning into her own chest as she witnesses this scene.*

Certainly, the references to the text are accurate, but what the writer is basically telling us is that she would rather analyze her own feelings than the text itself. She also has the audacity to claim that she knows what the reader feels as he or she reads the text. We have news for her: every reader is different and will react differently to text, so there is no point in discussing the reader. The scene she has chosen to write about is an apt one, but she needs to relate it more to the question about the outsider of society gaining a new perspective. Always make your literary essays about the literature.

## Strategy 9: Conclude by Reviewing and Re-Viewing

Once you have exhausted your text in the body of your essay, you must find a way to conclude. Too many writers will end with a brief paragraph that summarizes something that they have said before. We do not want to discourage this; it is important to review your main ideas in the conclusion. However, you shouldn't stop there. If you have time, you should not only summarize; you should also "re-view" your material— see it in a new way, revealing some new aspect of it based on what you have said in the body.

Let's compare the following two conclusions responding to the open question (see Strategy 8) using *The Scarlet Letter*:

*So, as stated before, Hester Prynne is an outsider. She is in exile from her society and can therefore look at them as through a microscope. She can see their flaws, their idiosyncrasies and their evils. She knows the truth about Dimmesdale, the truth about Chillingworth, and the truth about herself long before anyone else in her Puritan community does. In conclusion, when an individual lives outside of her society, she can know the truth about it.*

This conclusion is a competent review of what the writer has said before, but by the end, we are still only seeing what the prompt asked for; the writer hasn't discovered anything in her essay, only confirmed what she already knew.

*As an outsider, Hester has found the truth behind the cruelties of her fellow Puritans. She has also been privy to the secrets of her fellow outsiders: Dimmesdale and Chillingworth. However, because she has been outcast by a judgmental people, she no longer is obligated to come under their influence. In a way, her position as an outsider has helped her to maintain a personal integrity even though her neighbors would label her a sinner. By the end of Hawthorne's novel, Hester thus exerts more influence on her community than they do on her. On the Puritan perimeter, her patience, humility, hard work, and stoicism actually transform the meaning of the A from "adultery" to "able." Indeed, with her outsider's perspective, Hester is able to change an entire people from condemning and aloof to forgiving and tolerant.*

By contrast, this conclusion searches for something new. Without developing an entirely new thesis, this paragraph looks at what has already been said about the outsider's perspective and synthesizes a fresh pattern about communal influence, even supports this new concept with a reference to text. The result is a more authoritative and original essay.

# Strategy 10: Poetry Essay: Find the Sentences

Some readers complain that poems are difficult to read because they are written in verse. Even free verse is harder to read than a paragraph. However, if you search for the sentences in the poem, you can "straighten out" the verse in your head. For instance, in John Donne's 17th century poem "Legacy" listed below, if you look at the punctuation, you can see where the sentences end: lines 6, 8, 14, 16, 18, 20, 22a, 24.

When I died last, and, Dear, I die

    As often as from thee I go,

    Though it be but an hour ago,

And Lovers' hours be full of eternity,

5  I can remember yet, that I

    Something did say, and something did bestow;

Though I be dead, which sent me, I should be

Mine own executor[1] and Legacy.

I heard me say, "Tell her anon,

10   That my self (that is you, not I),

    Did kill me, and when I felt me die,

I bid me send my heart, when I was gone,

But I alas could there find none,

    When I had ripp'd me, and searched where hearts did lie;

15 It killed me again, that I who was still true,

    In life, in my last Will should cozen[2] you.

---

1.   *executer*: an administrator of a will

2.   *cozen*: trick, deceive

Yet I found something like a heart,

    But colors it, and corners had;

    It was not good, it was not bad,

20 It was entire to none, and few had part.

    As good as could be made by art

      It seemed; and therefore for our losses sad,

I meant to send this heart in stead of mine,

But oh, no man could hold it, for 'twas thine.


Written out as sentences, the poem would then look like this:

1. When I died last, and, Dear, I die as often as from thee I go, though it be but an hour ago, and Lovers' hours be full of eternity, I can remember yet, that I something did say, and something did bestow.

2. Though I be dead, which sent me, I should be mine own executor and Legacy.

3. I heard me say, "Tell her anon, that my self (that is you, not I), did kill me, and when I felt me die, I bid me send my heart, when I was gone, but I alas could there find none, when I had ripp'd me, and searched where hearts did lie.

4. It killed me again, that I who was still true, in life, in my last Will should cozen you.

5. Yet I found something like a heart, but colors it, and corners had.

6. It was not good; it was not bad.

7. It was entire to none, and few had part.

8. As good as could be made by art it seemed.

9. And therefore for our losses sad, I meant to send this heart instead of mine, but oh, no man could hold it, for 'twas thine.


The implication here is that if you can visualize these nine sentences, you will find nine complete ideas in the poem, and you are on your way to understanding the work better.

## Strategy 11: Poetry Essay: Reorder the Sentences

Poets like John Donne are fond of anastrophe, the poetic reordering of a sentence. Good poets use anastrophe to place emphasis on an important word. Bad poets use the device to make the meter and rhyme scheme of the poem work. The problem is that anastrophe can potentially ruin the casual reader's understanding of a poem. Thus, the next step in translating the poem is "de-anastrophizing" it. To that end, take a look at the more naturally ordered sentences from "Legacy" below:

1. When I died last, and, Dear, I die as often as <u>I go from thee</u>, though it be but an hour ago, and Lovers' hours be full of eternity, I can remember yet, <u>that I did say something, and did bestow something</u>.

2. <u>Though I, which sent me, be dead</u>, I should be mine own executor and Legacy.

3. I heard me say, "Tell her anon, that my self (that is you, not I), did kill me, and when I felt me die, I bid me send my heart, when I was gone, <u>but alas, when I had ripp'd me, and searched where hearts did lie, I could find none there</u>.

5. Yet I found something like a heart, <u>but it had colors and corners</u>.

8. <u>It seemed as good as could be made by art</u>.

9. And therefore <u>for our sad losses</u>, I meant to send this heart in stead of mine, but oh, no man could hold it, for 'twas thine.

You are now a little closer to a more contemporary translation of the text.

## Strategy 12: Poetry Essay: Translate from King James English, If Necessary

Again, the casual reader will have difficulty with older poems if he is not familiar with Elizabethan English. What follows is a quick "cheat sheet" to which you can refer if you need to brush up on your Renaissance-style language.

| | |
|---|---|
| **alas, alack** | too bad (Alas, I am undone. Alack, so art thou.) |
| **anon** | soon (I will call thee anon.) |
| **art** | are (Thou art a villain.) |
| **be** | am, is (I be angry with thee; it be an old wound) |
| **dost** | do (Thou dost make thine ears to fold.) |
| **doth** | does (He doth teach the caterpillars to wiggle.) |
| **hast** | have (Thou hast a large elbow.) |
| **hath** | has (She hath a pleasing scent.) |
| **thee** | you, usually as an object (I love thee.) |
| **thine** | yours, or your before a noun that starts with a vowel (My wagon is thine; thine eyes are bloodshot.) |
| **thou** | you, usually as a subject (Thou art a pig.) |
| **thy** | your (I loathe thy breath.) |
| **'twas** | it was ('Twas sad, alas.) |
| **wherefore** | why (Wherefore dost thou bite thine arm?) |

If we apply some of these translations to our now naturally ordered sentences from "Legacy," we get the following:

1. When I died last, and, Dear, I die as often as I leave you, though it is but an hour ago, and Lovers' hours are as long as eternity, I can remember yet, that I said something, and bestowed something on you.

2. Though I, who sent myself, am dead, I should be my own executor and legacy.

3. I heard myself say, "Tell her soon, that my self (that is you, not I), killed me, and when I felt myself die, I bid myself to send my heart, when I was gone, but too bad! when I had ripped myself, and searched where hearts usually lay, I could find none there.

4. It killed me again, that I who was still true, in life, in my last will should trick you.

5. Yet I found something like a heart, but it had colors and corners.

6. It was not good; it was not bad.

7. Nobody had all of it and few had any part of it.

8. It seemed as good as could be made by human effort.

9. And therefore for our sad losses, I meant to send this heart in place of mine, but oh, no man could hold it, because it was yours.

While our translation may have spoiled the "music" of the poem, it has also made it more manageable for analysis. Remember that you should only "correct" the poem in your head—not on the page. Be sure to keep in mind the original language, which may provide layers of meaning unavailable in your translation.

## Strategy 13: Prose Essay: Watch for Satire

You will not always find satire on the AP Literature Exam, but it pops up often—especially in the prose prompt—because satire offers many opportunities for writing about tone and purpose. However, many students who take the exam do not recognize satire, and therefore write poorly when a satirical piece appears in the prose question. How could this be?

If you're not expecting satire, it can disguise itself well. There is no "satirical tone"—often, satire is written in a serious tone. Plus, in an exam, satire comes out of context, so there are no "winks" or other clues that what you are reading is not intended seriously. Finally, the work might also be satirizing something unfamiliar, like 18th century society, so the point of the joke might not be apparent. Consider this passage from Jonathan Swift's "A Modest Proposal":

I have been assured by a very knowing American of my acquaintance in London, that a young healthy child well nursed is at a year old a most delicious, nourishing, and wholesome food, whether stewed, roasted, baked, or boiled; and I make no doubt that it will equally serve in a fricassee or a ragout.

5     I do therefore humbly offer it to public consideration that of the hundred and twenty thousand children already computed, twenty thousand

may be reserved for breed, whereof only one-fourth part to be males;
which is more than we allow to sheep, black cattle or swine; and my
10   reason is, that these children are seldom the fruits of marriage, a circumstance not much regarded by our savages, therefore one male will be
sufficient to serve four females. That the remaining hundred thousand
may, at a year old, be offered in the sale to the persons of quality and
fortune through the kingdom; always advising the mother to let them
15   suck plentifully in the last month, so as to render them plump and fat
for a good table. A child will make two dishes at an entertainment for
friends; and when the family dines alone, the fore or hind quarter will
make a reasonable dish, and seasoned with a little pepper or salt will be
very good boiled on the fourth day, especially in winter.

In this passage, Swift never winks at you to let you know he is kid-
ding. In fact, his tone is quite serious. And if you didn't know the context
that Swift was writing in—18th century Ireland—then you might not get
the joke.

So while misunderstanding satire is understandable, it will cost you
on the test. Our advice is to keep in mind the possibility that satire will
show up—if not in the prose prompt, then in the poetry question or possibly even in the multiple-choice section. What is the best way to look
for satire? Easy: as you read a passage that sounds serious, ask yourself if
the subject matter should be treated this way. If gravity doesn't seem to
be the right tone for the occasion, you may have satire on your hands.

## Strategy 14: Open Essay: Choose Wisely

In the open essay (the third essay), you will be given a list of about
twenty to thirty works, any of which can somehow be effective for the
prompt. Yet you can still choose the wrong work for this final writing
task if you aren't careful. Consider these factors:

**Base your choice on personal propriety:** All of the works from the list
will be appropriate for addressing the prompt, but many of them will

be inappropriate for *you*. There are some you haven't read, and perhaps others you started but never completed. There may be others that you have read but can't stand and would hate to write about, and still others that you love, but couldn't write about objectively—your emotions would get in the way, and you would want to talk about parts of the work that had nothing to do with the prompt. Therefore, you need to select a work you know well, but with which you can still manage some professional distance.

**Be original in your selection:** If you have your choices for the open question narrowed down to two works, and you think you could write just as well on either one, opt for the lesser known of the two. Think of the hundreds of thousands (yes, that many) of other test takers who are probably going to opt for the more familiar work. Think of that lone AP Reader from a community college in Texas who has already read twenty essays on that same work. Have mercy on her. She might read your essay with fresher eyes if you select the less commonly known work.

You can also abandon the suggested list and focus on another work that fits the question. If you do so, just be sure to choose complex, full-length literary works. Skip Shel Silverstein, Dr. Seuss, and the *Harry Potter* books.

# Mini-Diagnostic, Section I

Now it's time to put those strategies into practice. Let's start with a poem in the multiple choice section. This poem will be followed by ten questions. Try to finish in 10–12 minutes.

When I have seen by Time's fell hand defaced
The rich proud cost of outworn buried age,
When sometime lofty towers I see down-razed
And brass eternal slave to mortal rage[1];
5  When I have seen the hungry ocean gain
Advantage on the kingdom of the shore,
And the firm soil win of the wat'ry main,
Increasing store with loss and loss with store;
When I have seen such interchange of state,
10 Or state itself confounded[2] to decay,
Ruin hath taught me thus to ruminate,
That Time will come and take my love away.
    This thought is as a death, which cannot choose
    But weep to have that which it fears to lose.

---

1.   *mortal rage*: ravages of mortality
2.   *confounded*: reduced

1.  The speaker in the poem seems concerned with

    A.   a desire to control Time
    B.   nature's predictable changes
    C.   slavery's cold injustice
    D.   the kingdom's interchangeable politics
    E.   Time's destructive power

2.  The subject of the poem's first sentence is

    A.   "I" (line 1)
    B.   "cost" (line 2)
    C.   "Advantage" (line 6)
    D.   "store" (line 8)
    E.   "Ruin" (line 11)

3.  In lines 1–4, "rich proud cost," "lofty towers," and "brass eternal" all have which of the following in common?

    A.   They are images of political wealth.
    B.   They link the speaker to his past.
    C.   They become examples of ruin.
    D.   They demonstrate the process of order out of chaos.
    E.   They develop into military symbols.

4.  In lines 5–6, the ocean might be viewed as

    A.   an army of voracious soldiers.
    B.   a pair of hands caressing the shore
    C.   a group of diligent workers.
    D.   a collection of struggling poets
    E.   a court of foppish dandies

5.  The word "win" (line 7) in context probably means

    A.   try
    B.   triumph
    C.   gain

D. convince

E. achieve

6. The ocean image in lines 5–8 is unlike the images of lines 1–4 because it

A. describes an ongoing exchange while the others illustrate a sense of finality

B. attempts to mask the speaker's boredom while the others sound genuinely exciting

C. is an example of simile while the others show personification

D. interrupts the pedagogic flow of the poem while the others favor edification

E. develops a complaint about Nature while the others praise Nature's wonder

7. Lines 9–10 act as a

A. summary of previous lines

B. contradiction to previous lines

C. main theme for the whole poem

D. rhetorical question leading toward the conclusion

E. couplet in the sestet

8. In the final line, the word "weep" is used because the speaker

A. cannot accept the loss of his love

B. wishes to mirror the action of the ocean

C. fights against an unnatural force

D. cannot enjoy what he knows will not stay

E. is contemplating his own mortality

9. Which of the following does NOT appear in the final two lines?

A. antithesis

B. simile

C. personification

D. apostrophe

E. couplet rhyme

10. Throughout the poem, the speaker's tone seems to be

    A.   cheerful but understated

    B.   resolved but sad

    C.   lonely but hopeful

    D.   vulnerable but suspicious

    E.   antic but sober

## Answers for Questions 1–10

1. E. As usual, we can count on the first question to encompass the whole work. Readers who take a quick glance at the poem may reason that since Time is mentioned in the first line of the poem and also in answer A, that A must therefore be the right answer. Yet, if you look at the way the rest of the poem proceeds, you can see that Time has destructive power. It defaces (line 1), it razes towers (line 3), and it will eventually take the speaker's love away, presumably by overcoming the lover with old age and death (line 12). B is incorrect because although natural changes are brought up in the poem, they are not discussed as predictable; furthermore, "towers" and "brass" are artificial, so the poems' concerns go beyond the natural. C can't be right because it misreads the figurative language of line 4. E, therefore, is the correct answer.

2. E. Here we have an incremental question, one that is trying to teach something to you. If you can understand what the subject of the poem's first sentence is, then you can make more sense of the text, and thereby make more sense of the questions in this set. What the question is trying to get you to see is that the poem begins with a series of dependent clauses, all beginning with the word "when." They therefore can't contain the main subject of the sentence. Any subject that follows "when" ("I" in lines 1, 3, 5, and 9) would not be the main subject of the sentence, so we can eliminate A. Likewise, the nouns in B, C, and D are still located in the confines of those

"when" clauses, so they can be disregarded as well. Once the dependent clauses are eliminated, the first noun we see is "Ruin," so E is then correct. Now that we have the sentence structure of the poem figured out a little better, the successive questions shouldn't be as difficult to master.

3. **C.** When we say that Question 2 is incremental, we mean that it is a stepping stone to a succeeding question. Since we see in Question 2 that "Ruin" is the subject of the first sentence, and we remember that the poem as a whole concerns the destructive power of Time, then we can reason in Question 3 that "cost," "towers," and "brass" are examples of Time's ruinous effects. Time defaces cost (lines 1–2), razes towers (line 3) and ravages brass, perhaps with corrosion. Furthermore, when a question presents a list of items to you, you must pay attention to each item in the list. If you only look at "lofty towers," you might think that E is correct. Isolating "proud cost" and "brass eternal" might lead you to think that A is possible. B can be dismissed because the speaker is ruminating more about his future than his past. D is the weakest response, because the poem deals with just the opposite of what this option suggests.

4. **A.** The ocean is described as "hungry" in line 5, and A is the only one of the five answers to refer to hunger with the word "voracious." But there is more. Lines 5–6 see the ocean as gaining advantage on the shore's "kingdom." This image suggests an army advancing on an opposing country. The only other option that carries this much force is C, but the imagery of lines 5 and 6 makes this option too bland.

5. **C.** This is a vocabulary question. You know what the word "win" means, but in different contexts, that meaning may shift a little. So we have to consider what all the options here imply. A suggests that the soil is attempting to do something but not succeeding. However, line 8 indicates that the sea and the shore are engaged in a kind of give and take. So, at times, the soil is winning out. However, B seems

too strong a choice. Again, line 8 shows that the struggle between shoreline and ocean never ends, so neither side wins forever. D and E seem too weak to reflect this battle between earth and water. But C implies nothing permanent in the word "gain"; in fact, the word ties in with line 5 to remind us that the ocean and the land are operating in the same way.

6. **A.** The "rich proud cost" of line 2 is defaced without ever again being restored. The tower in line 3 is destroyed and not built back up. The brass in line 4 is corroded and remains so. Only in lines 5–8 do we see an ebb and flow between the land and the water. B and D are wrong because a test writer would almost never select a work in which the speaker sounded bored (B) or that seemed pedagogic (D); passages are selected because they seem intellectually stimulating, and B and D imply that there is something less than stimulating about the poem. C can't be right because the land and water in lines 5-8 are discussed literally; they aren't compared to something else figuratively, so there is no simile here, nor was there any use of personification in lines 1-4. Finally, although Nature is brought up in the poem, it is neither praised nor complained about.

7. **A.** The "interchange of state" in line 9 is a reference to the interaction between sea and shore. Examples of "state itself confounded to decay" would be, for instance, the tower and brass. Thus, the lines are summing up what has been said before. Instantly, A is right and B is wrong. The lines do not rhyme with each other, so E could not work. They do not form a question, so D is wrong. And since they do not form a complete idea, C is eliminated.

8. **D.** Lines 11 and 12 sound final and resigned. The speaker understands the evidence of lines 1–10 all too well: Time destroys everything. Therefore, he is in a state of acceptance and A is not a valid choice, no matter how apt it may have seemed at first. E may also seem like an attractive answer, because the mortality of the loved

one is being discussed, but the speaker in lines 13 and 14 sounds as though he expects to outlive his lover, thus the speaker isn't thinking of his own expiration date. Since Time is arguably a force of Nature, and also because the speaker does not seem to be putting up a fight against Time, C does not apply. B does not make much sense since all the ocean is doing is eroding the shore. So, we are left with D. Even though the lover is alive and present, one can infer that the fear of losing the lover prevents the speaker from enjoying their relationship.

9.  **D.** Antithesis (A) appears in the pairing of the opposites "have" and "lose" in line 14. The simile (B) occurs in line 13: "This thought is *as* a death…"; in other words, the thought of losing the lover is a kind of death for the speaker. The thought then goes on to "choose," "weep," "have," and "fear" (lines 13–14); these verbs personify (C) the thought, especially "weep." Of course, we see couplet rhyme (E) in the end words "choose" and "lose." But apostrophe? No. The speaker talks about Time, but not *to* it. Therefore, in this question we must choose the wrong answer, which is D.

10. **B.** Here, we have another question that reflects on the work as a whole. But there is also something different here. In this kind of question, if we can prove just one of the items in each option wrong, we can eliminate the entire option. At the thought of losing his lover, the speaker is definitely not cheerful; therefore, A is out. The speaker is also certain of losing his lover to Time; there is no hope here, and C then goes by the wayside. The certainty of the speaker goes beyond suspicion, so D is not strong enough to be a viable option. E is not correct because the steady pace and well-ordered complexity of the poem's sentence structure prevent the tone from being antic. However, the speaker is both accepting and sad about the loss of his love, so B is the correct option.

# Mini-Diagnostic, Section II

Next, try the multiple-choice strategies you learned on a prose passages. This passage is followed by 15 questions. Try to finish in 13–15 minutes.

[*The following passage comes from a short story taking place in the late 1960s. The speaker has wedded Mala—in an arranged marriage—but his education and profession have forced him to leave her in India, to live alone in London for a while, then to come to America. As the passage opens, Mala has recently joined him stateside.*]

At the end of the first week, on Friday, I suggested going out. Mala set down her knitting and disappeared into the bathroom. When she emerged I regretted the suggestion; she had put on a clean silk sari and extra bracelets, and coiled her hair with a flattering side part on top of
5   her head. She was prepared as if for a party, or at the very least for the cinema, but I had no such destination in mind. The evening air was balmy. We walked several blocks down Massachusetts Avenue, looking into the windows of restaurants and shops. Then, without thinking, I led her down the quiet street where for so many nights I had walked alone.
10     "This is where I lived before you came," I said, stopping at Mrs. Croft's chain-link fence.

"In such a big house?"

"I had a small room upstairs. At the back."

"Who else lives there?"

15    "A very old woman."

"With her family?"

"Alone."

"But who takes care of her?"

I opened the gate. "For the most part she takes care of herself."

20    I wondered if Mrs. Croft would remember me; I wondered if she had a new boarder to sit with her on the bench each evening. When I pressed the bell I expected the same long wait as that day of our first meeting, when I did not have a key. But this time the door was opened almost immediately, by Helen. Mrs. Croft was not sitting on the bench. The

25    bench was gone.

"Hello there," Helen said, smiling with her bright pink lips at Mala. "Mother's in the parlor. Will you be visiting awhile?"

"As you wish, madame."

"Then I think I'll run to the store, if you don't mind. She had a little

30    accident. We can't leave her alone these days, not even for a minute."

I locked the door after Helen and walked into the parlor. Mrs. Croft was lying flat on her back, her head on a peach-colored cushion, a thin white quilt spread over her body. Her hands were folded together on top of her chest. When she saw me she pointed to the sofa, and told

35    me to sit down. I took my place as directed, but Mala wandered over to the piano and sat on the bench, which was now positioned where it belonged.

"I broke my hip!" Mrs. Croft announced, as if no time had passed.

"Oh dear, madame."

40    "I fell off the bench!"

"I am so sorry, madame."

"It was the middle of the night! Do you know what I did, boy?"

I shook my head.

"I called the police!"

45    She stared up at the ceiling and grinned sedately, exposing a crowded row of long gray teeth. Not one was missing. "What do you say to that, boy?"

      As stunned as I was, I knew what I had to say. With no hesitation at all, I cried out, "Splendid!"

      Mala laughed then. Her voice was full of kindness, her eyes bright
50  with amusement. I had never heard her laugh before, and it was loud enough so that Mrs. Croft had heard, too. She turned to Mala and glared.

      "Who is she, boy?"

      "She is my wife, madame."

      Mrs. Croft pressed her head at an angle against the cushion to get a
55  better look. "Can you play the piano?"

      "No, madame," Mala replied.

      "Then stand up!"

      Mala rose to her feet, adjusting the end of her sari over her head and holding it close to her chest, and, for the first time since her ar-
60  rival, I felt sympathy. I remembered my first days in London, learning how to take the tube to Russell Square, riding an escalator for the first time, being unable to understand that when the man cried "piper" it meant "paper," being unable to decipher, for a whole year, that the conductor said "mind the gap" as the train pulled away from each sta-
65  tion. Like me, Mala had traveled far from home, not knowing where she was going, or what she would find, for no reason other than to be my wife. As strange as it seemed, I knew in my heart that one day her death would affect me, and stranger still, that mine would affect her. I wanted somehow to explain this to Mrs. Croft, who was still scru-
70  tinizing Mala from top to toe with what seemed to be placid disdain. I wondered if Mrs. Croft had ever seen a woman in a sari, with a dot painted on her forehead and bracelets stacked on her wrists. I wondered what she would object to. I wondered if she could see the red dye still vivid on Mala's feet, all but obscured by the bottom edge of
75  her sari. At last Mrs. Croft declared, with equal measures of disbelief and delight I knew well:

      "She is a perfect lady!"

Now it was I who laughed. I did so quietly, and Mrs. Croft did not hear me. But Mala had heard, and, for the first time, we looked at each
80  other and smiled.

Excerpt from "The Third and Final Continent" from *Interpreter of Maladies* by Jhumpa Lahiri. Copyright © 1999 by Jhumpa Lahiri. Reprinted by permission of Houghton Mifflin Harcourt Publishing Company. All rights reserved.

11. The meeting with Mrs. Croft would best be described as

    A.  worrisome and irritating
    B.  amusing and revealing
    C.  boring and empty
    D.  frustrating and saddening
    E.  sophisticated and elegant

12. If one considers lines 65–67, then the phrase "At the end of the first week" (line 1) refers to the first week of

    A.  Mrs. Croft's recuperation
    B.  being away from Mrs. Croft
    C.  Helen's stay with Mrs. Croft
    D.  the narrator's stay in a different country
    E.  the narrator and Mala's living together

13. In lines 1–6, Mala's preparations for going out and the narrator's subsequent regret about her appearance help to demonstrate

    A.  the unreasonable expectations that the narrator has for his new wife
    B.  the narrator's larger regret in marrying someone so unlike him
    C.  the first example of Mala's theatrical and self-indulgent nature
    D.  the couple's lack of communication and experience with each other
    E.  the types of problems that the couple will experience in their marriage

14. What do lines 10–23 NOT reveal about the narrator when he stayed with Mrs. Croft?

   A. He lived with Mrs. Croft before Mala arrived in Boston.
   B. Mrs. Croft and he were the only regular residents in her home.
   C. The narrator was not just a boarder but a caretaker for Mrs. Croft.
   D. It was customary for the narrator to sit with Mrs. Croft in the evening.
   E. When he first came to her door, Mrs. Croft took a while to answer.

15. In line 13, the narrator most likely wants to appear

   A. poor
   B. outcast
   C. complex
   D. unpretentious
   E. rebellious

16. When Helen says, "Mother's in the parlor," line 27, she dispels a possible expectation in line 24 that

   A. Mrs. Croft has moved
   B. Mrs. Croft does not wish to see the narrator
   C. Helen has bought the house from Mrs. Croft
   D. Helen has imposed her tastes on Mrs. Croft
   E. Mrs. Croft has died

17. In lines 35–36, what is the most likely reason Mala wandered "over to the piano" and "sat on the bench"?

   A. Mrs. Croft has directed her to do so.
   B. She is fearful of Mrs. Croft.
   C. The narrator has guided her to do so.
   D. She wants to display her musical abilities.
   E. She is still unfamiliar with her husband.

18. In the exchange between Mrs. Croft and the narrator (lines 38–48), the narrator appears

   A.   polite and eager to please

   B.   submissive and spineless

   C.   uncertain and cautious

   D.   hypocritical and obsequious

   E.   uncomfortable and anxious to leave

19. In the exchange between Mrs. Croft and the narrator (lines 38–48), Mrs. Croft appears

   A.   feeble and sickly

   B.   peremptory and vigorous

   C.   desperate and lonely

   D.   callous and aloof

   E.   awkward and insensitive

20. What causes the narrator to feel "sympathy" (line 60) when Mala stands?

   A.   He is reminded that she is overdressed for this simple occasion.

   B.   Mrs. Croft has awkwardly discovered that Mala has no talent for the piano.

   C.   He realizes that she must be tired after their long walk.

   D.   Mrs. Croft is inspecting her as a stranger and a foreigner.

   E.   He notices how uncomfortable Mala has been during the conversation.

21. In lines 60–65, the narrator speaks of his London experiences as

   A.   uncomfortable and confusing

   B.   angering and wild

   C.   adventurous and fun

   D.   loathsome and hurtful

   E.   orderly and monotonous

22. The greatest irony of lines 67–68 ("As strange as it seemed...would affect her.") is that

    A.  a young man would be thinking about his death in those surroundings

    B.  a person would be focusing on himself when there is an invalid in the room

    C.  a husband would think it strange that his death could affect his wife

    D.  a foreigner would consider his future when his present is so uncertain

    E.  an Indian would wonder about his marriage when he should accept the arrangement

23. The narrator's laugh in line 78 could plausibly have been brought on by all of the following EXCEPT

    A.  the affirmation that Mala is a "perfect lady" (line 77) after Mrs. Croft seemed to scrutinize Mala with "placid disdain" (line 70)

    B.  relief that Mrs. Croft, whom the narrator seems to respect, actually approves of Mala

    C.  a realization that despite their being largely unacquainted with each other, the narrator agrees with Mrs. Croft: Mala is a perfect lady

    D.  wonder that an old woman like Mrs. Croft could be progressive enough to recognize Mala as a perfect lady

    E.  the thought that Mala could be perceived as a perfect lady despite her physical appearance

24. By the end of the passage, a new connection between Mala and the narrator is evident in which of the following?

    I.    The way they smile at each other
    II.   Their shared dislike of Mrs. Croft's forwardness
    III.  The fact that Mala hears his laugh but Mrs. Croft does not
    IV.   The narrator's realization that they have shared the discomfort of being in a foreign place

    A. I only
    B. I, II, & III
    C. I, II, & IV
    D. I, III, & IV
    E. I, II, III, & IV

25. Which of the following is a possible theme that develops from the passage?

    A.   Arranged marriages are inferior to the process of choosing one's own mate.
    B.   Outsiders can sometimes help us to recognize the value of what we have.
    C.   Americans will never consider immigrants to be equals in the U.S.
    D.   We can learn a great deal from the elderly if we listen to them.
    E.   What is fated to fail in one country can actually succeed in another country.

## Answers to Questions 11–25

11. **B.** We can probably eliminate A and D immediately because the narrator and Mrs. Croft fall into their familiar, charming speech patterns right away; the experience seems neither irritating nor frustrating. Mala may be a little nervous at first, but her easy laughter during the conversation indicates that she is lightening up. Although some readers may feel bored reading the passage, it is not intended to be

boring. There is a tension at first in the meeting between Mrs. Croft, Mala, and the narrator, but then this tension opens up into a moment of discovery. C is therefore a poor choice. E doesn't seem viable, either. The unadorned setting of the parlor and the abrupt, bold statements of Mrs. Croft suggest an atmosphere that is less than sophisticated or elegant. However, both Mala and the speaker find amusement in this meeting, and the narrator discovers a deeper feeling for his new wife than he realized before, so B is the best option.

12. **E.** Lines 65–67 concern Mala and the speaker only, so the only options that could make any sense would be D and E. However, D leaves Mala out of the equation, so we must go with E. Another hint here is that one should always read the italicized introductory note at the beginning of a passage. In this case, the note offers information that confirms E's appropriateness.

13. **D.** The narrator has only proposed going out for a while. He has not stated any expectations of Mala. He does react negatively to her choice of clothing, but he has expressed no prior anticipation of what she should wear; A, then, is a misfire. B is also too broad an answer. The narrator may be disappointed in Mala's eveningwear, but that reaction does not lead to a regret of the entire marriage. Someone unfamiliar with the Indian sari may interpret Mala's clothing as theatrical and self-indulgent, but what she has put on is very traditional, very normal. Having recently arrived in America from India, she may also have no other type of clothes to wear. Thus, C is too judgmental and presumptuous. E also assumes too much, since the passage does not give us any insight into the speaker's future with Mala. If anything, by the end of the story excerpt, they seem to be connecting better. D is the only one in the question's set that bases its answer on what can be proven. The passage says that they have been together only one week. Mala's dressing up for a night out is simply an example of her inexperience with the narrator. He just wanted to go for a walk; she did

not know that was his intention. The two of them aren't used to communicating with each other, so they can misinterpret one another's messages.

14. **C.** The following is a list of lines that help to prove A, B, D, and E true:

> line 10: Option A
> lines 13–17: Option B
> lines 20–21: Option D
> lines 21–23: Option E

But what do we make of the narrator's statement, "For the most part she takes care of herself" (line 19)? Could we not infer that, if Mrs. Croft is capable of tending to herself "for the most part," someone else must take care of her "for the other part"? And might this caretaker be the narrator? The leaps in logic that we have to make here are too vast, especially when we see Helen, who runs to the store for Mrs. Croft, stays with her during her recuperation, and is thus the more likely candidate for caregiver. For this reason, C no longer looks tempting, and in this "EXCEPT" situation, we must choose this option.

15. **D.** To find the best response for this question, we need to make sense of the exchange between Mala and the narrator:

> "This is where I lived before you came," I said, stopping at
> Mrs. Croft's chain-link fence.
> "In such a big house?"
> "I had a small room upstairs. At the back."

Mala is emphasizing the large size of the house and the narrator is responding by making his quarters sound small and removed. But why would she care that the house is so big? If she is implying that the residence reflects wealth, then A is correct: as "small" is the opposite of "big," "poor" is the opposite of "wealthy." However, a "poor" room inside a "wealthy" house makes little sense. If the narrator is trying to make himself sound like an outcast (B), why would he recall the times he sat with Mrs. Croft on the piano bench? And if he wants to appear complex (C) why are Mala and he going out on a simple stroll through Boston, a date for which she is obviously, in his opinion, overdressed? Certainly, he does not want to appear rebellious (E) to Mala; he neither argues with her nor expresses a cross word in his conversation with Mrs. Croft. If we look at his behavior throughout the passage, the best response is D. Mala is surprised at the large size of the house, but the narrator reassures her that even though the house was big, he occupied only a small part of it. The narrator is stressing his unpretentiousness.

16. E. As the narrator is speaking to Mala about Mrs. Croft and reflecting on his time with the aged landlady, he fully expects to see her at her house. He wonders if she will remember him, if she has a new boarder, and so on. It never occurs to him that she would not want to see him, so we can toss out B. At the door, the narrator recognizes Helen right away and does not seem surprised by her presence; somehow, then, she has a connection with Mrs. Croft and seems to belong here. This familiarity can help us dispel A and C as options. Mrs. Croft's absence would also not be counted as a kind of interior design, so D is incorrect. What moves E to the forefront of these options is that the narrator has earlier remarked on Mrs. Croft's old age. In this context, when the narrator sees that Mrs. Croft is not occupying her usual areas of the house, we can infer that she has possibly died.

17. E. Starting in line 34, Mrs. Croft points the narrator to the couch and he silently sits. No one has directed Mala to do anything. It is her own idea to go sit on the bench. Immediately, we can dismiss A and C. Nowhere in the passage has she discussed her musical abilities, nor does she eye the piano with any sort of interest, so D is highly unlikely. B might be an attractive distracter, except that Mala "wanders"

over to the piano bench. This aimlessness does not betray any kind of fear of Mrs. Croft. However, we do know that Mala and the narrator have not spent much time together as husband and wife. There may be some discomfort here, so Mala is most likely heading for the bench to avoid an uncomfortable closeness with the narrator.

18. **A.** In this question, let's move from the least likely answer to the most likely answer. The narrator is not fidgety in Mrs. Croft's parlor; he isn't eyeing the door, coughing or giving other cues that he wants to leave, so we can safely assume that E is out. He does not flatter Mrs. Croft in any way, so we can leave out D; there are no obsequies in his speech, and he behaves with Mrs. Croft much as he did with Mala. One might read his brief responses to Mrs. Croft's conversation as a kind of uncertainty or caution, but he delivers his "Splendid!" with volume and immediacy, so C would be a troublesome answer. The most attractive distracter is B, because the narrator seems to be letting Mrs. Croft take control of the conversation. Yet, as deferential as he is, he is still not "spineless"; that word is too strong for his behavior. He does not mumble, stutter, stammer, bow his head, cower or do anything else that would connote weakness. Yet we can say that his address of Mrs. Croft as "madame" is polite, and that shouting out the word "Splendid!" has a kind of eagerness in it. A therefore seems the most reasonable answer.

19. **B.** We grant that Mrs. Croft is flat on her back with a broken hip, but the energy and optimism with which she speaks at once erase the possibility of either A or C. One might interpret her abruptness as callous and aloof (D), but line 75 ("She is a perfect lady!") deflates such an interpretation. Her politically incorrect use of the label "boy" for the narrator could be seen as awkward (E), but the narrator is not fazed by it, and Mala laughs kindly at his response to it. No one feels awkward here. The narrator and Mala may even feel grateful that Mrs. Croft forcefully takes control of the situation, which was probably more awkward before the couple arrived at

her house. There is no doubt, however, that Mrs. Croft's clipped phrasing is peremptory, or absolute, and her delivery is full of vigor, despite her injury. B is the best response.

20. **D.** When Mala stands, the narrator recalls what his life in London was like before he arrived in the U.S.: the difficulties in understanding British dialects, the uncertainty of living in a foreign land. He is reminded of these experiences because, as Mala is being scrutinized by Mrs. Croft, he remembers what it is like to be a foreigner (D). E is an attractive distracter because one would feel sympathy for someone if he noticed her discomfort, but the narrator here is more focused on his own memories than the way Mala has been feeling for the entire conversation. There is simply no evidence in the passage to support A, B, or C.

21. **A.** Lines 60–65 describe nothing positive about the narrator's London experience, so we can kick C out. Furthermore, his reaction to his time in Great Britain is fairly mild in retrospect. He repeats the word "unable" when remembering his attempt to cope with daily life, but "unable" is not a very emotional word; it falls short of either anger (B) or loathing (D). E may seem likely at first because the narrator talks about getting used to the phrases "piper" and "mind the gap" on a regular basis, but what keeps this experience from being monotonous is that he has a hard time figuring out what these expressions mean. Yet he is confused in London and his confusion presumably causes discomfort. Thus, A is correct.

22. **C.** If marriage is an official, lifelong commitment between two people, and one assumes that a marriage could last several decades until one of the spouses dies, it is logical to assume that the death of one spouse would somehow affect the other. Yet this thought is a revelation to the narrator. The irony stems from his lack of experience with Mala. She has been a stranger to him—like a foreigner in a new land—so he has not expected to feel any sense of loss if she were

to be out of his life. Yet this meeting with Mrs. Croft has caused him to sympathize with Mala, so much so that he is starting to think about her in the long term. As for A, why wouldn't someone contemplate death when an ancient woman lies prone recovering from a hip injury? Wouldn't death seem a natural association in this environment? D seems a bit insensitive: why would the question single the narrator out as a foreigner, when anyone could think about his future in an uncertain present. In fact, wouldn't some be inclined to think about their future if their present *is* so uncertain? B and E pass judgment on the narrator by implying that he should act in a certain way based on his background. Such bias goes beyond analysis; it takes us outside the text and can't be proven analytically.

23. **D.** In this EXCEPT question, A is plausible because, after displaying what looks like disdain, Mrs. Croft appears to approve of Mala. The narrator's laughter could be a reaction to this incongruity. Their conversation shows how much the narrator respects Mrs. Croft, so B could also work. Since the narrator has suddenly come to sympathize with Mala, he may view her with new appreciation; C also becomes possible. As Mrs. Croft studies Mala, the narrator wonders if the old woman notices certain aspects of his wife's appearance, such as the red dye on Mala's feet; such concern then makes E a reasonable choice. D seems to be the option to choose here, because it dismisses the former relationship between the narrator and Mrs. Croft. He ought to know whether Mrs. Croft is capable of appreciating Mala or not. To dismiss her as simply an "old woman"—and to make assumptions about the progressiveness of old women—does not sound like appropriate behavior for the narrator.

24. **D.** This is a new kind of EXCEPT question: the dreaded Roman Numeral Question. When the test maker creates an EXCEPT item, she sees four possible right answers and one wrong answer; it's up to us, then, to select the wrong answer. But in a Roman Numeral Question, there are usually only two or three responses that could

be right...so we have this troublesome construction in which we have to look at different answer combinations to see which one is the most solid.

So, ask yourself: in Question 24, does "I" seem right? Would two people smiling at each other indicate a connection? Yes, it would, so "I" remains as a possibility. Do Mala and the narrator share a dislike of Mrs. Croft's forwardness? Doubtful. They both seem to enjoy her enthusiasm. "II" is out. The fact that Mala picks up on the narrator's laughter shows that she is paying attention to him, whereas Mrs. Croft is not as keyed in; "III" is now a contender. "IV" also seems right because the word "shared" certainly suggests a connection between Mala and her husband. We then select D since it alone contains the combination of I, III, and IV.

25. **B.** Even though you may believe A to be true, this passage portrays the narrator and Mala as capable of deep feelings for one another, and they are part of an arranged marriage. No comparison is made to any other sort of marriage, so A is doubly wrong. If you see Mrs. Croft as a biased American who treats Indians with some disdain, you still can't choose C because the passage makes no attempt to generalize Mrs. Croft into the typical American; nor does the excerpt try to make any predictions about American immigration attitudes. D is wrong, because although Mrs. Croft has asked questions and made declarations, she has given no advice. E assumes too much; there is no telling, based on what we see in the passage, that the marriage between Mala and the narrator would have failed if they had lived in Great Britain or India. B, though, is aware of Mrs. Croft as a foreign catalyst—however accidental—for getting the narrator to appreciate something he had not earlier seen in Mala.

Had this been an *actual* testing situation, you would have had about thirty more multiple-choice questions to answer.

# Mini-Diagnostic, Section III: The First Essay

I n the final diagnostic, you can put the essay strategies you learned into action by writing a poetry essay. Try to finish in 40 minutes.

Read the following poem very carefully. Then, write a well-organized essay in which you explain how the poem encourages an appreciation of nature. You may include—but are not restricted to—imagery, sound devices, narrative shifts, and parallelism.

The Fish, the Man and the Spirit

*To a Fish*

You strange, astonished-looking, angle-faced,

Dreary-mouthed, gaping wretches of the sea,

Gulping salt-water everlastingly,

Cold-blooded, though with red your blood be graced,

5  And mute, though dwellers in the roaring waste[1];

And you, all shapes beside, that fishy be—

Some round, some flat, some long, all devilry,

Legless, unloving, infamously chaste—

O scaly, slippery wet, swift, staring wights,[1]

10 What is't ye do? What life lead? Eh, dull goggles?

How do ye vary your vile days and nights?

How pass your Sundays? Are ye still but joggles

In ceaseless wash? Still nought but gapes, and bites,

And drinks, and stares, diversified with boggles[2]?


### A Fish Answers

15 Amazing monster! That, for aught I know,

With the first sight of thee didst make our race

Forever stare! Oh flat and shocking face,

Grimly divided from the breast below!

Thou that on dry land horribly dost go

20 With a split body and ridiculous pace,

Prong after prong, disgracer of all grace,

Long-useless-finned, haired upright, unwet, slow!


O breather of unbreathable, sword-sharp air,

How canst exist? How bear thyself, thou dry

25 And dreary sloth? What particle canst share

Of the only blessed life, the watery?

I sometimes see of ye an actual *pair*

Go by! Linked fin by fin! odiously.


### The Fish Turns Into a Man, and Then Into a Spirit, and Again Speaks

Indulge thy smiling scorn, if smiling still,

30 O man! And loathe, but with a sort of love;

For difference must its use by difference prove,

And in such sweet clang, the spheres with music fill.

One of the spirits am I, that at his will

Live in whate'er has life—fish, eagle, dove—

---

1     *wights:* creatures

2     *boggles:* sudden movements

35 No hate, no pride, beneath nought, nor above,

   A visitor of the rounds of God's sweet skill.

   Man's life is warm, glad, sad, 'twixt loves and graves,

   Boundless in hope, honored with pangs austere,

   Heaven-gazing; and his angel-wings he craves:

40 The fish is swift, small-needing, vague yet clear,

   A cold, sweet, silver life, wrapped in round waves,

   Quickened with touches of transporting fear.

                                                          (1836)

[First, apply essay strategies 1–12 to the prompt above, then write a well-developed response. Try to stay within a 40-minute time limit. Next, compare your response to the samples below.]

## The "9" Response: Convincing and Sophisticated

A man stands on a sandy beach. He stares out and spies a lone fish leaping among the ocean waves. Yet the man does not wonder at the small creature's beauty. Instead, he is repulsed by the fish and berates it. Surprisingly, the fish returns fire and denigrates the man. Such is the unlikely situation in Leigh Hunt's "The Fish, the Man and the Spirit." In the war of words between these two characters, it becomes clear that a rigid self-orientation prevents the man from appreciating the fish's place in Nature and vice versa. Hunt's poem develops these narrow-minded positions using both sound devices and reductive imagery.

Among the many insults delivered by the man is this description of all fish: "O scaly, slippery wet, swift, staring wights/What is't ye do? What life lead?" (lines 9–10). The rhetorical questions strongly indicate that fish are inferior to humanity because they lack a human sense of purpose, but what may be a subtler device here is the speaker's alliterated "s" in line 9. On the one hand, the repeated initial "s" could mimic the fish's splashing in the sea, but more pertinently, the repetitive sound connotes that fish are all alike in their lowliness. The fish, too, uses alliteration that places humans in a state of debased "otherness": "Amazing monster!

That for aught I know/With the first sight of thee didst make our race/ Forever stare! Oh flat and shocking face…!" (lines 15–17). The repeated F in line 17 could signify our respiration "of unbreathable, sword-sharp air" (line 23), but it also reflects the fish's interpretation of humans as a collectively "unfishy" and therefore substandard species. Thus, both the man and the fish stereotype each other through sound.

If this notion seems a bit far-fetched, then a more convincing discussion may lie in the visual images that each creature uses to debase the other. The fish, for instance, is appalled at the duality of our physiognomy. We are "Grimly divided from the breast below" with a "split body and ridiculous pace" that proceeds "Prong after prong" (lines 18–21). Furthermore, we have a tendency to think doubly in our social behavior: "I sometimes see of ye an actual pair/Go by! Linked fin by fin! odiously" (lines 27–28). What could be wrong with these images of "doubleness," except that they are foreign to the fish, who is singular in his lack of division? We are distasteful to him only because we are unlike him. Similarly, the man hates the fact that the fish has no human trait. He uses synecdoche to reduce all fish to a series of fragments. The creatures are "nought but gapes, and bites/And drinks, and stares, diversified with boggles" (lines 13–14). These images not only focus on the nonhuman actions and appearance of the fish, but they also view fish as incomplete beings. Neither the man nor the fish can respect the other creature for what it is; in fact, both beings disrespect each other for being so alien.

The fish therefore, inexplicably, becomes a spirit so that its dispute with the man can be resolved. As an omniscient creature, it now understands that "difference must its use by difference prove" (line 31): instead of trying to analyze all of Nature with a species-centered microscope, we should see the beauty and usefulness of Nature's diversity, proof of "God's sweet skill" in creation (line 36). And if we learn to appreciate the differences among all creatures, we may ultimately come around to the similarities we share. As the last stanza explains, humans may be "Boundless in hope" (line 38), different from fish who are characterized more by "touches of transporting fear" (line 42). Yet both species, in their own way, are marked by a desire for more; the fish is "small-needing" (line 40) but not so unlike the larger human, whose "Heaven-gazing" (line 39) also indicates need. In a sense, Hunt suggests that embracing Nature's differences will unveil the world's beauty and paradoxically reveal to us our kinship with all creatures.

### Why This is an Upper-Level Essay

Let's move chronologically through the essay and view it in terms of some of the strategies we have already presented.

### Strategy 4: A Well-Balanced Introduction

In terms of length, this intro would make Goldilocks very happy; it is "just right," neither too short nor too long. More importantly, it stays focused on the text. There are no unnecessary references to the history of humans and fish or complaints about our society today being too shortsighted to appreciate our dwindling natural resources. The first paragraph simply sums up what takes place in the poem and uses that summary to segue into its thesis, which links sound devices and imagery to the prejudices of the fish and the man. What moves this introduction from merely "well-written" to "sophisticated" is the imaginative context in which it places the fish and the man. By providing a "sandy beach" setting, the writer makes the conversation between human and fish more concrete without moving too far outside the text.

### Strategy 5: Give Directions to the Reader

In the last sentence of the introduction, we know that the writer is going to correlate the small-mindedness of the fish and the man with visual and auditory imagery. Yet the writer doesn't tip his entire hand. For instance, he doesn't explain in detail what the significance of such a link would be. He is going to let the body of the essay develop that significance and then find a new way to view that significance in the conclusion. If he announced all of his moves up front, the intro would become too long and there would be nothing left to figure out as the essay progressed.

## Strategy 6: Use Good Examples

Are the writer's examples appropriate? Yes—he consistently quotes text that supports his position. Furthermore, whereas less skilled writers might spend too much time summarizing what they have quoted, this writer is more concerned with *applying* what he has quoted to his argument, showing *how* the quote supports his main idea rather than uselessly rehashing the lines of the poem.

Are his examples varied? Yes again—in two ways. First, he focuses on sound devices like alliteration, then he discusses more visual types of imagery like synecdoche. Second, he varies the presentation of each device by providing examples from both the man's view and the fish's.

Are his examples original? Not many readers would see a tie between a repeated "s" sound and a human's prejudices against fish. This part of his argument may be stretched a little thin ("9" essays don't have to be perfect), but he certainly gets points for trying a fresh approach. There is something else to note here: the writer doesn't just tag these devices as if he is playing a game of hide and seek; rather, he is explaining why these particular figures of speech are so appropriate to the unity of Hunt's work. The important idea is *not* that synecdoche is in the poem, but that synecdoche is an effective way to show a fragmented, dehumanized picture of the fish, to make it look inferior to humans.

## Strategy 7: Organize Your Points Climactically

First, the writer discusses sound devices, then moves on to visual images. Why not organize things the opposite way? The answer lies in the first sentence of the third paragraph. The writer has admitted here that this part of his thesis may not be very convincing, so he is now going to launch into a more persuasive piece of evidence. In other words, he is moving from the weaker part of his argument to a stronger part. He is therefore organizing his points climactically.

Another noteworthy aspect of his organization is that the writer does not give in to an unsophisticated chronological approach. The line numbers of his quoted evidence jump around in the poem, because he is basing his organization topically. He therefore sees some parts of the poem as more pertinent to his discussion. This approach is much more discerning and analytical than merely talking about the poem stanza by stanza.

### Strategy 8: Avoid Discussing the Reader

The word "reader" never enters into this essay, for example, in a sentence such as "The reader becomes annoyed that the fish and the man can't work out their differences." Instead, from start to finish, the writer stays wholly focused on what the text has to say. An essay which remains reader-focused seems to be hiding its uncertainty about the text. If you are telling us what the reader thinks about the poem, you aren't telling us about the poem.

But what about the writer's occasional use of first person plural, in such sentences like, "Furthermore, we have a tendency to think doubly in our social behavior"? Isn't this an instance of discussing the reader without naming the reader? A clever observation—but no. Whenever this essay uses any form of "we" it is discussing humans, the way they are perceived in the poem. In other words, "we" are not readers, but subjects of the work. The first person plural is therefore fair game in the essay.

And for the record: use no synonyms of the word "reader" in your essay. Phrases like "the audience," "someone looking at this poem," or "the literary community" take us just as far outside the text as the phrase "the reader" does.

### Strategy 9: Conclude by Reviewing and Re-Viewing

A host of student writers are going to finish their essays with conclusions that just summarize what they have already said. The typical topic sentence for this kind of conclusion is, "Overall, the alliteration and synecdoche of the poem prove that the man and the fish do not see eye to eye on each other's existence." Most of the essay has already covered this ground. These writers have definitely "reviewed" their material with us, but not "re-viewed" it—seen it in a new light. Not so the writer of our "9" essay.

The last sentence of the third paragraph and the first sentence of the last paragraph join together in reviewing what has already been noted about the man and the fish:

> "Neither the man nor the fish can respect the other creature for what it is;
> in fact, both beings disrespect each other for being so alien.
> The fish therefore, inexplicably, becomes a spirit so that its dispute
> with the man can be resolved."

However, the writer uses this review to set up two new ideas. The first is that the poem encourages all creatures to appreciate Nature's differences. With this "re-viewing" out of the way, why go on? Hasn't the essay already done what it needed to do? Actually, it hasn't. This new idea is only a summary of the last stanza. The end of the poem needs to be mentioned, but it doesn't count as an original conclusion. Therefore, the writer goes on to discover a paradox: that a respect for the differences in Nature will help humans to see the similarities they share with other beings in the world. This revelation builds on what has already been developed in the essay, but doesn't take us in such a completely different direction that we have to write more paragraphs to explain it. The essay thus ends in as balanced a manner as it began.

Now, let's look at a response that hits the middle range of essays.

## The "5" Response: Plausible and Competent

Throughout the ages, human beings have been in conflict with fish. We catch them, eat them, pollute their habitats and make them feel unwanted. You'd think that we were the crowning achievement of the world from the way that we treat fish, as though they were not as important as we are. In Leigh Hunt's 1836 masterpiece, "The Fish, the Man and the Spirit," he uses imagery, sound devices, narrative shifts, and parallelism to show that we all need to appreciate Nature just a little bit more.

First, Hunt uses imagery: "You strange, astonished-looking, angle-faced/Dreary-mouthed, gaping wretches of the sea/Gulping salt-water everlastingly/Cold-blooded, though with red your blood be graced/And mute, though dwellers in the roaring waste/And you, all shapes beside, that fishy be—/Some round, some flat, some long, all devilry" (lines 1–7). In this quote, the man is astonished at the way that fish look. They are dreary things that gulp sea water, and even though they have red blood in their veins, the blood is cold, not like humans. Clearly the speaker does not like fish and does not appreciate Nature.

Second, Hunt uses sound devices: "O scaly, slippery wet, swift, staring wights/What is't ye do? What life lead? Eh, dull goggles?/How do ye vary your vile days and nights?/How pass your Sundays? Are ye still but joggles/In ceaseless wash? Still nought but gapes and bites/And drinks, and stares, diversified with boggles?" (lines 9–14). In line 9, the reader can see alliteration being used. Four words in the line start with the letter "s." This slows the reader down a little bit and really makes her look at the line and pay attention to it. Plus, "scaly" and "staring" don't sound very complimentary. Again, the man is not appreciating Nature the way that he should.

There are also narrative shifts in the poem. First, the man talks, then the fish, then the fish becomes a spirit and finishes the poem. When the man and the fish are talking, all they do is insult each other. "O scaly, slippery wet, swift, staring wights/What is't ye do? What life lead? Eh, dull goggles?" (lines 9–10) says the man. The fish responds with just as much venom: "Amazing monster! That for aught I know/With the first sight of thee didst make our race/Forever stare! Oh flat and shocking face/Grimly divided from the breast below!/Thou that on dry land horribly dost go/With a split body and ridiculous pace/Prong after prong, disgracer of all grace…" (lines 15–21). Neither of them likes their looks or behavior. The man wants the fish to look and act like a human, and the fish wants humans to be more like fish. But when the fish changes into a spirit, it suddenly understands that we should learn to appreciate Nature by appreciating the differences in Nature: "Indulge thy smiling scorn, if smiling still/O man! And loathe, but with a sort of love/For difference must its use by difference prove/And in such sweet clang, the spheres with music fill" (lines 29–32). Therefore, narrative shifts help to show that we can appreciate Nature if we see its differences, unlike the man and the fish do.

Finally, parallelism is in the poem: "Man's life is warm, glad, sad, 'twixt loves and graves/Boundless in hope, honored with pangs austere/Heaven-gazing; and his angel-wings he craves;/The fish is swift, small-needing, vague yet clear/A cold, sweet silver life, wrapped in round waves/Quickened with touches of transporting fear" (lines 37–42). In this last stanza, there is parallelism between the man and the fish. The first three lines talk about what life is like for the man. The last three lines talk about the fish's life. There are many similarities here.

So, in conclusion, when the man and the fish argue, they do not understand each other's differences. But when the fish changes, the two of them can start to see that their differences are a good thing. In Leigh Hunt's poem, he is saying that we can appreciate Nature when we appreciate differences. Hunt makes this clear with imagery, sound devices, narrative shifts, and parallelism.

We are now going to comment on this response in the same way that we tackled the "9" essay earlier. However, before we begin, we want to point out a surprising aspect of this "5": it contains 10 more words than the "9," two more paragraphs, and it still scores four points lower. The lesson? A long essay doesn't guarantee a high score. You can pad your paragraphs until the cows come home and you aren't necessarily going to get your response into the 7-8-9 range. Beware.

### Why This Is a Middle-Level Essay
### Strategy 4: A Well-Balanced Introduction

As far as length goes, this introduction isn't bad. It doesn't wander around for too long and actually allows time to funnel down to its thesis. However, there are still at least four things wrong with this first paragraph.

The first is that it starts out far too broadly, trying to scan "the ages" (which could be a few millennia) and condense them into a couple of sentences. Our recommendation is not to rely on history for your introduction; the mantra is "stay in the text."

The second problem stems from the first: the writer has started with such a big scope that when she needs to get to her thesis, she can't find a smooth transition. Look how abrupt the break is between sentences in the fifth line of the essay. There is no cohesion here.

The thesis sentence ("In Leigh Hunt's masterpiece...") presents the next problem. It gushes unnecessarily over the poem by calling it a masterpiece. Who cares if the poem is great or not? Just analyze it. There is also an awkward construction in the main subject and verb: "he uses." The pronoun "he" doesn't have an antecedent because the phrase "Leigh Hunt's" is not a noun, but a modifier for "masterpiece." The sentence would begin better this way: "Leigh Hunt's 1836 poem "The Fish, the Man and the Spirit" uses..."

Finally, this writer is unimaginatively rephrasing the prompt and incorporating it into her thesis. The writer of the "9" essay was more discerning by selecting two of the proposed elements and expanding on each. The "5" writer indiscriminately throws all four elements of the prompt in her introduction and hopes that she is being thorough. In fact, just the opposite is true.

## Strategy 5: Give Just Enough Direction

If you look at the writer's thesis, you see that she is going to prove how four different elements of the poem emphasize the necessity of appreciating nature. By the end of the essay, she hasn't found anything beyond this idea. She has left no room for surprises, so our journey through her response is steady, but a tad bland.

## Strategy 6: Use Good Examples

One reason why the writer's examples are not fully appropriate is that she quotes far too much text. If she includes five lines in a quote, she may only discuss one line. Another problem with appropriateness is that, even though she grasps the general meaning of each stanza, she spends far too much time summarizing what she has quoted. There is no need for rehash. After you quote, you need to discuss the excerpt's unique relation to your thesis.

There is variety in the essay's examples, but each of the four elements being analyzed here is given only one quotation. The response therefore lacks depth; it skims across the surface of the poem rather than trying to explore one or two elements more fully.

By lifting the prompt into her thesis, the writer displays no originality. She even discusses the four recommended elements in the order that the prompt presented them.

### Strategy 7: Organize Your Points Climactically

Unskillfully, the writer moves chronologically through the poem. As a result, she may not have chosen the best examples for each element that she analyzes. To her credit, she does cover the entire poem, but not in any insightful way.

### Strategy 8: Avoid Discussing the Reader

The third paragraph offers us this unhelpful observation: "Four words in the line start with the letter 's.' This slows the reader down a little bit and really makes her look at the line and pay attention to it." The writer needs to tell us how the alliteration functions in the poem, not what the device is doing to the reader. Remember to always focus on the text.

### Strategy 9: Conclude by Reviewing and Re-Viewing

If you examine the writer's final paragraph, you see that there is no new idea presented. The conclusion basically summarizes what was brought up way back in the introduction. Instead of taking us on a scenic trek through the mountains, this essay has just been running in place.

# Glossary

Following is a list of defined terms that often appear on the AP Literature Exam, either in the multiple-choice questions or in essay prompts. These terms may be of further use to you when you write your essay responses for the test. However, be cautious: simply mentioning the terms is not as impressive as explaining how they are being used in a text and why they are so appropriate for creating meaning in the context of a passage.

**Agon**
In a narrative, an episode of conflict, usually between two characters. Beowulf is said to be divided into three agons: Beowulf vs. Grendel, Beowulf vs. Grendel's mother, and Beowulf vs. the dragon.

**Allegory**
Narrative in which the characters, setting, and events are all symbolic. Bunyan's *Pilgrim's Progress* tells the story of Christian, who journeys to Celestial City while wearing a great bundle on his back. The narrative allegorizes a Christian individual who is burdened by sin but wants to reach Heaven.

| | |
|---|---|
| **Alliteration** | Device in which the initial sound of a word is repeated at least twice in a line of poetry or in a sentence. Example: Chris kissed Karen, who clocked him convincingly. |
| **Allusion** | In a literary work, a reference to something appearing elsewhere in history, culture, or literature. Example: Edmund talked his sister into paying him for the privilege of rubbing his feet. That boy is a regular Tom Sawyer. |
| **Ambiguity** | Stylistic approach in a literary work whereby the text's lack of clarity allows for multiple, even conflicting interpretations. In the final scene of the 2010 film *Inception*, the central character spins a top to see whether he is dreaming or not. If the top continues to spin, he is dreaming; if it falls, he is awake. The film ends before the wobbling top has a chance to fall. |
| **Anachronism** | A character, object, or event placed in an incorrect period of time, like a Honda Civic showing up in poem about the Civil War |
| **Analogy** | A resemblance drawn between two items. A science professor may create an analogy between the collapse of a star and the crumpling of a piece of paper to discuss the concept of implosion. |
| **Anaphora** | The repetition of a word or phrase for rhetorical effect. Example: <br><br> I love your eyes <br> I love your nose <br> I love the way you spread your toes. |

**Anastrophe**            The inversion of a sentence's normal word order, usually used in poetry to reassign emphasis. In the *Star Wars* saga, Yoda constantly speaks in anastrophic phrases: "Help you I can, yes," instead of "Yes, I can help you."

**Antagonist**            The opponent of a narrative's protagonist or hero. The antagonist can sometimes be called the villain of a story, but not all antagonists are villainous. Because she is in conflict with the protagonist McMurphy about hospital policy, Nurse Ratched is the antagonist of Kesey's *One Flew Over the Cuckoo's Nest*.

**Anticlimax**            A sudden decline in tension, especially with comic effect or ironic disappointment. Example: Bombs fell around Johnson's head. Bullets whizzed past his ears. He felt the screams of agony from his fellow soldiers. Suddenly, he reached inside his backpack, groped in its dark interiors, and withdrew a crossword puzzle.

**Antihero**              A protagonist with villainous qualities who nevertheless can be relatively sympathetic in a narrative. Satan in Milton's *Paradise Lost* is an example.

**Antithesis**            Statement in which two opposites are paired to make a point. When he descended the ladder of the Apollo module and touched the lunar surface, Neil Armstrong said: "That's one *small* step for [a] man, one *giant* leap for mankind."

**Antonym**               A word that has the opposite meaning of another. "Sacred" is an antonym for "profane."

| | |
|---|---|
| **Aphorism** | A clever, brief observation about some aspect of life, also called a maxim or a saying. Franklin's "A penny saved is a penny earned" is an aphorism. |
| **Apostrophe** | An address to something as if it were human, or an address to someone not present. Example: Hello, you beautiful little tofu burger. I can't wait to eat you. You look so scrumptious. Example II: (With your mother at home, as you rifle through your purse on the school bus) MOM! Why didn't you put my phone in my purse? |
| **Archetype** | A symbol so ancient and fundamental that its meaning is understood by the unconscious mind, even without contextual explanation. In many cultures, the moon is an archetype for feminine power, change, and the seasons. |
| **Assonance** | The repetition of a vowel sound in a sentence or line of poetry. The repetition does not have to occur in the initial position of a word, as with alliteration. Example: The can of apples sat on the veranda. |
| **Avant-garde** | French for "vanguard," a term pertaining to edgy, innovative, nontraditional works of art and literature. In the 1930s, much abstract art was considered avant-garde because it broke with previous traditions of realism. |
| **Ballad** | Type of poem usually featuring four-line stanzas written in an ABCB rhyme scheme with alternating iambic tetrameter and trimeter lines. Example: Sir Horsbreath found the dragon's cave And readied for attack. |

He pulled his rusted broadsword out
And gulped his dinner back.

**Blank verse**     Unrhymed iambic pentameter verse—formal, but still conversational. Example:
Aunt Edna likes to swallow playing cards
Then cough them up for kids on holidays.

**Caesura**     A pause in the middle of a line of poetry. Example:
The Vikings sailed. They headed West
To slay some goats, then wed the rest.
(The caesuras occur after "sailed" and "goats.")

**Canto**     Long section of an epic poem. A canto is to a poem what a chapter is to a novel.

**Catharsis**     According to Aristotle, the audience's release of pity and fear once the tragic hero of a play has experienced a downfall. In Sophocles' *Oedipus Rex*, once Oedipus emerges onstage with his eyes gouged out, the audience experiences catharsis.

**Character**     An agent committing action in a narrative, usually human, but not necessarily so, as seen in Orwell's *Animal Farm*. Below is a list of different character types:

*dynamic*     Experiences a change in personality, attitude, or behavior during the course of the narrative

*flat*     Underdeveloped character, one-dimensional and predictable

*round*     More developed, complex character

*static*     Character that remains the same throughout a work

| | |
|---|---|
| **Chiasmus** | A statement or passage made up of balanced parts that undergo a reversal. Snoop Dogg's "[I've got] my mind on my money/And my money on my mind" is an example. |
| **Climax** | In a narrative, the point of irreversible action, when what is done cannot be undone. When Juliet stabs herself in the family crypt, we have reached a climactic moment. |
| **Comedy** | A play in which a temporarily unstable situation is restored to order by the end. Comedies are usually humorous but do not have to be. |
| **Conceit** | An extended metaphor continuing from an initial comparison. Example: My love for you is a wildebeest. It drinks from the watering hole of your heart. It endures like the beast's curved horns, hardened by trial and maturation. |
| **Connotation** | The implied, rather than direct meaning of a word. "Thin" and "emaciated" are synonyms, but "emaciated" connotes an unhealthy sort of thinness. |
| **Consonance** | The repetition of consonant sounds in a sentence or line of poetry. This repetition does not have to occur in the initial position of words. Example: The puppet trapped the yipping puppy in a pipe. |
| **Couplet** | In a poem, two consecutive rhyming lines. Example: <br> In outer space, there lives a frog <br> Who chases spaceships like a dog. |

**Denouement**    French for "unknotting," this final segment of a narrative follows the climax and "winds things up" in the story. In the denouement of *The Great Gatsby*, Nick attends Gatsby's funeral, breaks up with Jordan, and philosophizes about the American Dream.

**Diction**    Word choice; the most basic element of a text. Diction can reveal a speaker's tone, or attitude toward her subject.

**Dissonance**    Harsh, unpleasant sounds, especially in poetry. Example:

The staccato clank of forks against cheap stemware
Recalled Bette to reality, catastrophically.
She had to pucker up and kiss
That sweating shyster, that advocate
Of corporate takeovers: Bill,
That blubbering husband.

**Dramatic monologue**    Poem in which a character speaks as if delivering a soliloquy. Tennyson's "Ulysses" and Browning's "My Last Duchess" are Examples.

**Enjambment**    A line of poetry that continues its sentence into the next line without a break. Example without enjambment:

The bee is camping in my hair.
I feel it making s'mores up there.

Example with enjambment:

The bee is scouting out a site
Where it can build a tent at night
Upon my newly stylized do
That took an hour to wash, or two.

| | |
|---|---|
| **Epic poem** | Long narrative poem, usually featuring a larger-than-life hero who takes a journey during which he receives divine intervention. *Gilgamesh*, *The Iliad*, *The Divine Comedy*, and *Paradise Lost* are all examples. |
| **Exposition** | Part of a narrative during which characters, setting, and initial action are explained. A good bulk of a story's exposition takes place near the beginning. |
| **Falling action** | Part of a narrative that moves from the climax to the denouement. |
| **Farce** | Absurd type of comedy that involves flat characters, slapstick action, and ridiculous misunderstandings. The Three Stooges and the Marx Brothers' films were often farcical. |
| **Figurative language** | See "imagery." |
| **Flashback** | Narrative scene in which action previously unrevealed takes place. An adult character's current motivation may be explained in a flashback returning to a traumatic event in his childhood. |
| **Foreshadowing** | A narrative event that, in retrospect, symbolically predicted something in the narrative's future. The witches' predictions for Macbeth make little sense until the events play out later in Shakespeare's tragedy. |
| **Frame narrative** | A story within a story. Chaucer's *The Canterbury Tales* is an example. The outer story involves a group of pilgrims heading for Canterbury during |

Eastertide, but each pilgrim is directed to tell a story on the way there and on the way back.

**Free verse**    Poetry with no rhyme or set meter. Whitman's *Leaves of Grass* is an example.

**Hero/heroine**    The protagonist of a narrative. This central character does not need to possess typically heroic characteristics. Creon in Sophocles' *Antigone* is a hardheaded bully, but is largely regarded as the tragic hero of the play.

**Hubris**    Common tragic flaw of protagonists. "Hubris" translates from the Greek as "pride," the kind of pride that makes a character foolishly think he is on par with the gods. In Shakespeare's play *Julius Caesar*, Caesar himself has this kind of prideful ego.

**Hyperbole**    Exaggeration for effect. "He had a swimming pool as big as the ocean."

**Iamb**    The most common metrical foot in English poetry. It consists of two syllables, the second one accented. The name "Marie" is an example of an iamb.

**Iambic pentameter**    The most common meter in English poetry One line of iambic pentameter has five ("penta") iambs, or roughly ten syllables with the accents on the even syllables. Romeo's monologue in Act II scene ii of *Shakespeare's Romeo and Juliet* clearly exemplifies this rhythm:
But SOFT! What LIGHT through YONder WINdow BREAKS?

| | |
|---|---|
| **Idyll** | Poem that idealizes rural life or a previous time. Tennyson's *Idylls of the King*, about the glory days of Camelot, is an example. |
| **Imagery** | Any description that appeals to the senses. Devices such as metaphors, similes, personification, and hyperbole are types of imagery. |
| **In medias res** | Latin for "in the middle of things." Many narratives, including epic poems, start *in medias res*. Later in the story, through flashbacks and exposition, we find out what has led up to this point. |
| **Invocation** | A plea or prayer to the Muse for a blessing on the poet's work—usually elaborated on for several lines in an epic. Byron parodies the technique in his mock epic *Don Juan*, when he writes "Hail, Muse, etc...." |
| **Irony** | An unexpected but fitting twist in a narrative. Irony typically falls into three categories: |
| *verbal* | Occurs when someone means the opposite of what she says. Example: Sandra walked off the plane in a frazzle. Her hair was matted down, her mascara ran into her crow's feet, and tiny globs of bread from the on-flight hoagie had become wedged in her front teeth. At the gate, her sister Eileen raised an eyebrow and said, "Honey, you've never looked better!" |
| *situational* | Occurs when events in a story take an unexpected turn, but one can still understand how the events could have happened. In O. Henry's "The Gift of the Magi," an impoverished husband sells his watch at Christmas to afford new combs for his wife's |

hair. However, at the end, we find out that she has sold her hair to buy him a new watch fob. Meh. It's the thought that counts.

*dramatic*  Occurs when the audience knows something that a character doesn't (a common device in suspense stories and horror movies). In *Eight-Legged Freaks*, a man watches television, oblivious to the fact that a gigantic spider is crawling up the back of his chair and is about to devour him.

**Local color**  Description of a specific region of country, so specific that the land and customs of the region are not likely duplicated anywhere else. Twain's *The Adventures of Huckleberry Finn* is full of local color that describes the topography and inhabitants of various Southern states during the early 19th century.

**Meiosis**  Understatement, the opposite of exaggeration. Example: The Milky Way galaxy is a pretty big place.

**Metaphor**  A direct comparison of two unlike things. Example: The earth is a tortoise clambering around the sun.

**Meter**  The set, repeated rhythm of a poem. If meter is not accompanied by rhyme, the poem is said to be blank verse. Without meter or rhyme, the poem is free verse.

**Metonymy**  Occurs when something associated with a thing represents that thing. Example I: In a monarchy, everyone is expected to obey the crown. (In this case, "the crown" stands for a human ruler. It would be silly to obey a crown literally. What's a crown going to tell you to do?). Example II: Have you read Dickinson before? (Does Emily Dickinson have words written on her? In this case, "Dickinson," the name, stands for the poetry written by Emily Dickinson.)

**Mock epic**    Satirical work that parodies the form of the epic poem. Pope's *The Rape of the Lock* is an example.

**Monologue**    Speech delivered by a character in a play, usually with other characters present. In Shakespeare's *Hamlet*, King Claudius' opening monologue is like a State of the Union address.

**Mood**    The emotional atmosphere of a work, especially the emotional undercurrents of a setting. Not to be confused with tone, which, though emotional, has more to do with the speaker's attitude. Horror writers like Edgar Allan Poe and Stephen King starkly evoke mood in their narratives.

**Motif**    A recurring pattern of images and symbols. A myriad of blood images resolve into a motif in Shakespeare's *Macbeth*, while a motif of armlessness (dress dummies, statues, etc.) weaves its way through Irving's *A Prayer for Owen Meany*.

**Novel**    A long, sustained work of narrative fiction, usually divided into chapters. DeFoe is often credited with writing the first novel in English, *Robinson Crusoe*, but the novel existed even before he was published in the 1600s.

**Novella**    A relatively brief novel, usually not exceeding 200 pages. Conrad's *Heart of Darkness* is an example.

**Ode**

A poem of praise and dedication. An example is Keats' "Ode on a Grecian Urn," in which he glorifies a vase's beauty.

**Oxymoron**

A seemingly self-contradictory term or phrase. Some oxymorons are "jumbo shrimp" and "loving hate."

**Parable**

A brief, symbolic story whose purpose is to instruct. In the Christian Testament, Jesus often taught using parables such as "The Prodigal Son."

**Paradox**

A seemingly self-contradictory statement that upon closer scrutiny actually reveals a truth. Wordsworth's "My Heart Leaps Up When I Behold" contains this famous paradox: "The Child is father of the Man." In other words, what we do and say as children shapes us in our adult lives.

**Parody**

A work that mocks another text by closely modeling its style and content. In the title sequence of the Adult Swim animated series *Robot Chicken*, four texts are parodied. A dead chicken lies in a road until a white-haired mad scientist picks it up, takes it back to his castle laboratory, and turns it into a cyborg who is then strapped into a chair and, while its eyes are pried open by pincers, forced to watch multiple television screens. The scene recalls the "Why did the chicken cross the road?" riddle, the 1931 film *Frankenstein*, the *Star Trek: Next Generation* television series (especially the Borg episodes), and the 1971 film *A Clockwork Orange*.

| | |
|---|---|
| **Pastiche** | A work that pays homage or responds to another work by closely mimicking its style and content. Raleigh's "The Nymph's Reply to the Shepherd" is a pastiche of Marlowe's "The Passionate Shepherd to His Love." |
| **Pastoral** | A poem that glorifies the beauty of nature and the lives of farmers, shepherds, and other bucolic folk. Virgil's *Eclogues* is an example. |
| **Personification** | The instilling of human characteristics in something nonhuman. Example: The flowers are rallying against my allergy medication (rallying is a verb associated with humans). |
| **Play** | A work of prose or poetry intended for performance on a stage. Comedies, tragedies, and melodramas are the most common types of plays. |
| **Plot** | The sequential action of a narrative; what "happens" in a story; what the characters "do." In a nutshell, the plot of *Snow White* can be summarized as follows: a beautiful girl, in trying to escape a queen jealous of her beauty, finds a cottage where seven little men live. She hides out with them for a while until the queen finds her and, disguised as an old woman, gives her a poisoned apple. The girl falls into a deep sleep until a prince comes along, kisses her, wakes her from her sleep, and carries her off to his castle. Luckily, the queen has been destroyed by this time, so the prince and the girl can live happily ever after. |
| **Poem** | A work written in verse rather than prose. This is probably the oldest of all literary forms. |

**Point of view**    The perspective from which a narrative is told. The point of view may be that of a character in the story (first person) or from a narrator removed from the story's events (third person) who may even know the thoughts and feelings of the characters (omniscient). Ishiguro's *Remains of the Day* is an example of first person narration, as the narrative is delivered by the protagonist Stevens, the butler of a British lord in the 1930s. Hardy's *Jude the Obscure* is told from a third person omniscient point of view, so that the narrator knows the thoughts of all the characters in the novel.

**Proem**    Abbreviated prose work featuring devices and language that make the text sound much like a poem. Forche's disturbing "The Colonel" is an example.

**Prose**    Any literary work that is not poetry, but is written in sentences and paragraphs. Novels, short stories, plays, and essays are just a few examples of prose works.

**Protagonist**    The central character of a literary work. Hester Prynne is the protagonist of Hawthorne's *The Scarlet Letter*.

**Quatrain**    A sequence of four lines in a poem, usually an English sonnet. The quatrain features some kind of rhyme scheme. Example:
Injected with a hormone in its back,
The duck began to ripple on the slab;
The walls reverberated with its quack,
So out I went and drove off in my cab.

| | |
|---|---|
| **Rhyme** | Usually, the repetition of final sounds in words at set intervals. Below are listed different types of rhyme: |
| *end rhyme* | Appears at the end of a line of poetry, the most common type of rhyme |
| *internal rhyme* | Appears within one line of poetry |
| *rhyme scheme* | The pattern of rhyme occurring in a poem, usually listed as a sequence of alphabetical letters (e.g. ABABCDCDEFEFGG) in which like letters indicate end rhyme |
| *slant rhyme* | Also called "near rhyme," words at the ends of poem lines that almost but don't quite rhyme. Not necessarily a weakness in the poem. |
| **Rhythm** | The pattern of stressed and unstressed syllables in a line of poetry that leads to a meter. See "meter." |
| **Rising action** | Appears after the exposition of a narrative. In this part of a story, complications begin to arise for the characters. In Shakespeare's *Hamlet*, for instance, the rising action begins when the ghost of the prince's father commands Hamlet to murder Claudius. |
| **Satire** | Comic work in which the foibles of society are addressed and mocked. Much of what takes place on the television comedy shows *Saturday Night Live* and *The Colbert Report* is satire. The most famous literary satire is probably Swift's "A Modest Proposal," in which he addresses the dilemma of Irish poverty and famine by suggesting that the English eat Irish babies and thereby create a new source of revenue for Ireland. |

**Setting**    The time and place of a narrative. In science fiction, for instance, the setting is sometimes a future Earth, an alien world, or a spaceship on a long journey.

**Short story**    A brief work of fictional prose invented roughly in the early 1800s. Short stories are often published in collections because of their brief length.

**Simile**    An indirect comparison between two unlike things. The comparison usually hinges on the word "like" or "as." Forrest Gump's, "Life is like a box of chocolates" is an example.

**Sonnet**    A poetic closed form devised during the early Renaissance by the Italian writer Petrarch. A sonnet consists of 14 lines, contains an intricate rhyme scheme, and discusses an idea rather than telling a story.
*Italian (Petrarchan) sonnet* divides its discussion between an octave (first eight lines) and a sestet (last six lines).
*English (Elizabethan) sonnet* divides its discussion among three quatrains and a final couplet.

**Sprung rhythm**    Distinctive, purposefully mixed or uneven meter in a poem, usually associated with the work of Gerard Manley Hopkins. "God's Grandeur" is an example.

**Stage directions**    Usually appearing in bracketed italics in a play's text. Stage directions explain how the stage is set, where and when the actors should move, and, occasionally, in what manner the actors should deliver their lines.

| | |
|---|---|
| **Stream of consciousness** | Type of narration that mimics the mind's free flow of thought. A seemingly disorganized point of view, stream of consciousness seeks to add greater realism to a narrative. Porter's "The Jilting of Granny Weatherall" and Joyce's *Ulysses* are examples. |
| **Syllepsis** | Expression in which both a literal and a figurative predicate split from a single verb phrase. Example: Harry should have gone to the prom with Diana. It turns out that she cleaned up beautifully when she wasn't playing softball. That night, he *ate steak for dinner and humble pie for dessert.* |
| **Symbol** | An object, setting, event, or flat character that represents an idea. Whereas a *sign* stands for a single, simplified concept (a red octagonal sign at a four-way intersection means "stop"), a symbol relies on a more complex context to create meaning, and often can mean different things in different situations. The scarlet A in Hawthorne's *The Scarlet Letter*, for instance, originally stands for adultery," but by the end of the novel, takes on the meaning of "able." |
| **Synesthesia** | A poetic blending of sensory images. Example:<br>The purple tunes were wildly sung;<br>I tasted half notes on my tongue. |
| **Synecdoche** | Imagery in which the part stands for the whole or vice versa. Example: The law chased Irving down the alley. Here, the whole—law—represents a single police officer or group of officers chasing down a perp.) |

**Theme**　　　　　　The universal truth, observation about life, or main idea of a literary work. The plot tells you what happens in a narrative, but the theme provides the meaning of that action. In the plot of Fitzgerald's *The Great Gatsby*, a bootlegger tries to win back the love of an old girlfriend. One theme derived from this plot might be that reliving the past is a futile act, because we have changed so much in the present.

**Tone**　　　　　　The narrator's attitude toward her subject. In Chopin's "The Story of an Hour," one can determine from the diction of the work that the narrator's tone is wry and ironic.

**Tragedy**　　　　　Play in which the protagonist makes a judgment error caused by a personality defect. This flaw then leads to his or her downfall by the end of the play. In Miller's *Death of a Salesman*, Willie's denial of reality leads to his estrangement from his sons and his eventual inability to cope with the decline of his career.

**Tragic flaw**　　　　The personality defect that leads the tragic hero in a play to make an error in judgment. Othello's pride, credulity, and blind temper cause him to kill his wife unjustly in Shakespeare's play. This error then leads to Othello's death.

**Understatement**　　See "meiosis."

**Verisimilitude**　　　The elements of a work that blend to make it believable and real. Presentational theater purposefully rejects verisimilitude; this kind of drama never wants the audience to forget that it is watching a play. Thus, it can be argued that presentational theater is more honest than other art forms, because it is not trying to lie to the audience.

**Zeugma**        See "syllepsis."

# THE BIG PICTURE: HOW TO PREPARE YEAR-ROUND

Have you picked up this guide for the AP Literature Exam months in advance of exam time? Then we applaud your initiative. But while it may seem like you have all the time in the world to prepare, it's best to get a head start now and start preparing. This section will cover:

- How to register for the test

- How to prepare in class

- How to prepare outside class

- Other things you can do to prepare

When you finish reading this section, a great sense of calm should wash over you, because you have not only the time but also the necessary knowledge to prepare daily for taking the AP Literature Exam.

## Registering for the Exam

The first step to take for registration is to visit College Board's "AP Central" website (www.apcentral.collegeboard.com) to get info about exam dates, fees, waivers, and the like.

If information hasn't been provided by your English teacher, talk to a guidance counselor about your school's policies for registering and paying exam fees. In most cases, your counselor will have the forms necessary for you to fill out. If she doesn't, she can direct you to the right person or location.

### Which Tests Should You Take?

High school can be a juggling act. Between your challenging classes, extracurricular activities, and the many distractions available outside of school, many students wind up sleep deprived and, perhaps, and wondering just why they signed up for so much punishment at the beginning of the year. If that describes you, take a realistic look at your schedule for the coming year. If you know which college you'll be attending, find out which AP exams can earn you college credit. Prioritize those that you think you'll have the best shot at, and those that can earn you credit.

If you're not taking an AP English class, you can still take the exam and do well. Many students earn high scores by studying on their own. If you have an aptitude for writing and know your way around a work of literature, you should be in position for a successful exam. Just take a practice test to get an idea of what you're in for, follow the advice in this section, and use the rest of the book to help you prepare for the exam. If you are still applying to colleges, they will be impressed by your ambition, and if you're graduating this year, you'll be glad to be ahead of the game if you can earn college credit.

### Don't Confuse the Two AP English Tests!

Don't forget that AP offers two English tests—the English Literature Exam and the AP English Language Exam. Make sure that you sign up for and sit the correct exam. Unless you are preparing for both exams simultaneously, you will not be ready for the Language Exam. The AP Literature Exam tests knowledge and abilities that relate to "imaginative" works including of fiction and poetry. The Language Exam tests your ability to read and write about nonfiction works. Many a student has mistakenly signed up for the wrong exam, wasting countless hours of study.

## Having Second Thoughts?

It's common to worry about receiving a low score on an AP exam, and sometimes tempting to skip it altogether. Maybe your nerves have temporarily gotten the better of you or you feel inadequately prepared. Take a deep breath and think again. Aside from the registration fee, you don't have much to lose.

If you are worried about your score, don't be. Admissions officers are more likely to be impressed that you took the test than they are to penalize you for a low score. And, especially if you took AP English, a low score is better than no score. If you're in your senior year and know which college you'll be attending, you really have nothing to lose, except for the college credit you might earn by taking the test.

If you're lacking in confidence, don't underestimate what you know. You do not have to be able to answer every question accurately to earn a respectable score on the multiple-choice section. If you're a good writer, then you should be able to perform well on the essays. Unlike many AP exams, the English Literature Exam is a skills-based exam, which means that it's more of a test of how well you do something than a test of what you know. All that you need to be able to do is understand and analyze a piece of literature. You don't have to memorize a formula or stuff your head with knowledge.

## Preparing in Class

It's hard to adopt the mentality that the way you study every day in your AP class affects the outcome of the exam—but it's true. Sometimes, students conveniently forget that the daily grind sharpens them into test-taking ninjas. Look at the following list and see what is missing from your daily regimen:

1. **Take notes every day.** Never leave a class without taking some notes. Even if the teacher isn't lecturing, even if the class is only having a discussion, take notes—definitions of terms on the left, summary notes on the right. More importantly, review those notes at the end of the week. Too many students, especially seniors, have such busy schedules that they forget what happens from one day to the next. Reviewing your notes will fill in those gaps.

2. **Participate.** Engage in class discussion. Ask questions. If you aren't participating, you won't be paying attention. If you aren't paying attention, how can you learn?

3. **Do the homework.** Yes, *all* of it. When you skip the parts that seem unimportant, you create little chinks in your education, little gaps in your brick wall of knowledge. If you skip enough homework, that wall will come tumbling down.

4. **Clarify feedback.** Did you get a paper back from your teacher with a less-than-stellar grade on it? Do you understand why? If not, check in with him. Conference. Conference anyway, even if you do understand the grades. Remove the mystery from class expectations. Ask how you can be a better learner.

5. **Be original.** Try to tackle assignments in ways that other people aren't, but still follow the assignment directions. A fresh approach can lead to greater perspective.

6. **Read actively.** When you read a novel, don't just read to find out what's going on. Look for deeper meaning, just as you would when you read a passage in the AP exam. Get into the habit of reading with a pen in hand, and (assuming you own the book) marking it as you read. That doesn't mean underlining half the book—just be ready to jot the occasional note in the margin. Perhaps you note a recurring theme, sense a shift in tone, or grasp a hidden meaning

in a line of dialogue. Writing down your thoughts will help clarify them in your head, and give you a guide for when your go back over the text later.

## Preparing Outside of Class

Learning doesn't stop when the last bell rings. It's what you do outside of class that matters most. Here are some things you can do to make the most of your out-of-class time between now and the exam.

1. **Organize your after-school schedule.** School ends for the day. Sometime later, you hit the pillow for a good night's rest. In between, you have some homework to do, and a few other activities. Carve out enough time for yourself so that you can get the homework done. Figure out the best, most *consistent* time of day for you to get everything finished. If necessary, reward your efforts with a snack, a TV show, a downloaded tune, or a trip to the mall.

2. **Limit distractions.** Some people tell themselves they can multitask by texting, chatting, watching TV, checking e-mail, and listening to music while they work. In reality, multitasking is a myth. The human brain can only focus on one thing at a time, so "multitasking" is really just switching tasks. And the more times you switch tasks, the more time you have to spend refocusing on the task at hand. That's even more true when you're reading challenging literature. You'll save countless hours, and absorb much more, if you set aside distractions and focus for a few hours at a time on your reading and other schoolwork.

3. **Organize your homework.** You know best which courses bore you to tears and which ones rev your motor. So what does that mean for the order in which you do your homework? Do you do your favorite class first because it will give you the initial momentum you need to sail through the rest of your work? Or do you save it for last, as a kind of treat waiting for you? Figure it out!

4. **Read and write for fun.** The more you read and write for enjoyment, the more proficient you will become. Of course, not all reading and writing are created equal. You'll get less benefit from texting a friend (though you may learn to be less wordy) than you will from thoughtful journaling or blogging. Reading a literary author you enjoy will get you farther than reading a fluff magazine. The important thing is to find something challenging enough that it will sharpen your mind, but fun enough that you'll actually do it during your free time.

## Reading Lists

If you are interested in reading more substantive works to prepare for the challenges of the AP Literature Exam, then try something from one of the lists below. These works are the sort of thing you might come across in the exam, but probably won't be reading in class:

**16th Century**

a sonnet cycle (e.g., *The Amoretti* by Edmund Spenser)

Thomas More's *Utopia*

a play by one of Shakespeare's contemporaries (e.g., Philip Marlowe's *Dido, Queen of Carthage*)

**17th Century**

metaphysical poetry by someone other than John Donne (e.g., George Herbert's "The Pulley")

Miltonian poetry other than *Paradise Lost* or his sonnets (e.g., *Samson Agonistes*)

Daniel Defoe's *Robinson Crusoe*

a Restoration play (e.g., William Wycherley's *The Country Wife*)

the poems of Edward Taylor

## 18th Century

a satirical novel (e.g., Smollett's *Humphrey Clinker*)

Jonathan Swift's *Gulliver's Travels*

Samuel Dryden's poetry and essays

Alexander Pope's poetry

the poetry of Phillis Wheatley

## 19th Century

Lord Byron's *Childe Harold*

Anne Brontë's *The Tenant of Wildfell Hall*

George Eliot's *The Mill on the Floss*

Alfred, Lord Tennyson's *Idylls of the King*

Herman Melville's *White Jacket*

Nathaniel Hawthorne's *Blithedale Romance*

Mark Twain's *Letters from the Earth*

the poetry of Paul Laurence Dunbar

## 20th and 21st Century

T. S. Eliot's *Murder in the Cathedral*

Joseph Conrad's *Lord Jim*

Richard Wright's *Native Son*

the short fiction of Saki

the short fiction of Katherine Anne Porter

Saul Bellow's *Henderson the Rain King*

Sinclair Lewis' *Babbitt*

Samuel Beckett's *Endgame*

Kazuo Ishiguro's *Remains of the Day*

Toni Morrison's *Tar Baby*

Michel Chabon's *The Amazing Adventures of Kavalier and Clay*

the poetry of Billy Collins

This list is woefully incomplete but would keep even the fleetest of readers occupied for a while.

# Resources for Further Study

**www.mymaxscore.com/aptests**  At this site, you can take another free AP practice test. Detailed answers and explanations are provided for both the multiple choice and essay sections.

**www.collegeboard.com**  The College Board's official site contains a wealth of advice on taking the exam, as well as sample multiple-choice and essay questions. It also shows you the essay questions for exams over the last several years. At the College Board's store, you can purchase full exams from past years, including sample essay responses and the scores they earned.

**Test Prep Books**  There are many additional test prep books that can offer more tips as well as additional practice tests. The Princeton Review, Barron's, Kaplan, and McGraw-Hill all offer worthwhile guides, if you have the time.

If you want to supplement your reading of this guide with another text, probably the best bet is to pick up one of the College Board's "Released Exam" volumes. You'll find real AP Literature tests that have actually been used in past years.

This book contains one practice test. Visit mymaxscore.com
to download your free second practice test with
answers and explanations.

# AP English Literature and Composition Practice Exam

## Section I
### Time: 1 hour

**Directions:** This section includes selections from literary works, followed
by questions about their form, content, and style. After reading each
selection, choose the best answer to each question. Pay particular attention to questions that contain the words NOT, LEAST, or EXCEPT.

**Questions 1–10. Read the following poem carefully before choosing
your answers.**

### Anniversary

Suppose I took out a slender ketch[1] from
under the pokes of Palace pier[2] tonight to
catch a sea going fish for you

---

1    *ketch:* two-masted boat

2    Palace pier was an emporium built on Brighton Beach in Sussex, England, and
featured arcades, concessions and souvenir shops.

or dressed in antique goggles and wings and

5  flew down through sycamore leaves into the park

or luminescent through some planetary strike

put one delicate flamingo leg over the sill of your lab

Could I surprise you? or would you insist on

keeping a pattern to link every transfiguration?

10  Listen, I shall have to whisper it

into your heart directly: we are all

supernatural / every day

we rise new creatures / cannot be predicted

"Anniversary" from *Collected Poems and Translations* by Elaine Feinstein, (c) 2002 Carcanet Press Limited.

1.  The speaker in the poem probably most enjoys

    A.  consistency
    B.  spontaneity
    C.  chaos
    D.  eloquence
    E.  praise

2.  The poem's addressee is best viewed as

    A.  an orderly scientist
    B.  a reflective historian
    C.  a talented musician
    D.  a playful teacher
    E.  an arrogant doctor

3.  The speaker's proposal in the first stanza can be described as all of the following EXCEPT

    A.  considerate
    B.  purposeful
    C.  desperate
    D.  detailed
    E.  lighthearted

4.  Compared to the speaker's proposal in the first stanza, the one she makes in the second is more

    A.  serious
    B.  prosaic
    C.  destructive
    D.  mellow
    E.  fantastic

5.  The third stanza features elements that contrast

    A.  the astounding and the silly
    B.  the natural and the artificial
    C.  the young and the old
    D.  the rare and the commonplace
    E.  the extreme and the bland

6.  In line 9, the phrase "every transfiguration" refers to

    A.  the various formulae analyzed by the addressee
    B.  the addressee's attempts to change the speaker's identity
    C.  the speaker's frustrations in communicating with the addressee
    D.  the speaker's attempts to surprise the addressee
    E.  the past disagreements between the speaker and the addressee

7.  The "it" of line 10 is

    A.  a transfiguration
    B.  a point about human randomness
    C.  an affirmation of the values held by the addressee
    D.  a reminder of a shared experience between the speaker and the addressee
    E.  a plea for the end of conflict between the narrator and the addressee

8.  In lines 10–13, the speaker wishes to do all of the following EXCEPT

    A.  link her previous proposals to an overall theme
    B.  correct a misperception held by the addressee
    C.  appeal to the addressee's emotions
    D.  shame the addressee into seeing her point
    E.  change her volume to communicate more effectively

9.  The fragmentation of the poem's stanzas and the slashes (/) in lines 12–13 exemplify

    A.  the addressee's attitude
    B.  the speaker's message
    C.  "a pattern" mentioned in line 9
    D.  a decay in the speaker's coherence
    E.  a lack of craft in the poem's composition

**Questions 10–28. Read the following passage carefully before choosing your answers.**

[In the following passage, taken from a British novel published in 1854, a classroom of children is being addressed by three men. The first is Thomas Gradgrind, who is something of a headmaster for the school. The second is M'Choakumchild, a newly trained teacher. The third, who begins the passage, is a government official. The class's newest student is Cecilia "Sissy" Jupe, who is trying to get accustomed to her new surroundings.]

'Suppose you were going to carpet a room. Would you use a carpet having a representation of flowers upon it?'

There being a general conviction by this time that 'No, sir!' was always the right answer to this gentleman, the chorus of NO was very
5  strong. Only a few feeble stragglers said Yes: among them Sissy Jupe.

'Girl number twenty,' said the gentleman, smiling in the calm strength of knowledge.

Sissy blushed, and stood up.

'So you would carpet your room—or your husband's room, if you
10 were a grown woman, and had a husband—with representations of flowers, would you?' said the gentleman.

'Why would you?'

'If you please, sir, I am very fond of flowers,' returned the girl.

'And is that why you would put tables and chairs upon them, and
15 have people walking over them with heavy boots?'

'It wouldn't hurt them, sir. They wouldn't crush and wither, if you please, sir. They would be the pictures of what was very pretty and pleasant, and I would fancy—'

'Ay, ay, ay! But you mustn't fancy,' cried the gentleman, quite elated
20 by coming so happily to his point. 'That's it! You are never to fancy.'

'You are not, Cecilia Jupe,' Thomas Gradgrind solemnly repeated, 'to do anything of that kind.'

'Fact, fact, fact!' said the gentleman. And 'Fact, fact, fact!' repeated Thomas Gradgrind.

25  'You are to be in all things regulated and governed,' said the gentleman, 'by fact. We hope to have, before long, a board of fact, composed of commissioners of fact, who will force the people to be a people of fact, and of nothing but fact. You must discard the word Fancy altogether. You have nothing to do with it. You are not to have, in any object of
30 use or ornament, what would be a contradiction in fact. You don't walk upon flowers in fact; you cannot be allowed to walk upon flowers in carpets. You don't find that foreign birds and butterflies come and perch upon your crockery; you cannot be permitted to paint foreign birds and

butterflies upon your crockery. You never meet with quadrupeds going
35 up and down walls; you must not have quadrupeds represented upon
walls. You must use,' said the gentleman, 'for all these purposes, combinations and modifications (in primary colours) of mathematical figures
which are susceptible of proof and demonstration. This is the new discovery. This is fact. This is taste.'

40 The girl curtseyed, and sat down. She was very young, and she
looked as if she were frightened by the matter-of-fact prospect the
world afforded.

'Now, if Mr M'Choakumchild,' said the gentleman, 'will proceed to
give his first lesson here, Mr Gradgrind, I shall be happy, at your request,
45 to observe his mode of procedure.'

Mr Gradgrind was much obliged. 'Mr M'Choakumchild, we only wait
for you.'

So, Mr M'Choakumchild began in his best manner. He and some
one hundred and forty other schoolmasters, had been lately turned at
50 the same time, in the same factory, on the same principles, like so many
pianoforte[1] legs. He had been put through an immense variety of paces,
and had answered volumes of head-breaking questions. Orthography,
etymology, syntax, and prosody, biography, astronomy, geography, and
general cosmography, the sciences of compound proportion, algebra,
55 land-surveying and levelling, vocal music, and drawing from models,
were all at the ends of his ten chilled fingers. He had worked his stony
way into Her Majesty's most Honourable Privy Council's Schedule B[2],
and had taken the bloom off the higher branches of mathematics and
physical science, French, German, Latin, and Greek. He knew all about
60 all the Water Sheds of all the world (whatever they are), and all the
histories of all the peoples, and all the names of all the rivers and mountains, and all the productions, manners, and customs of all the countries,
and all their boundaries and bearings on the two and thirty points of the

---

1    *pianoforte:* formal name for a piano

2    *Her Majesty's...Schedule B:* rigorous government training to certify teachers

compass. Ah, rather overdone, M'Choakumchild. If he had only learnt a
65  little less, how infinitely better he might have taught much more!

He went to work in this preparatory lesson, not unlike Morgiana in
the Forty Thieves[3]: looking into all the vessels ranged before him, one
after another, to see what they contained. Say, good M'Choakumchild.
When from thy boiling store, thou shalt fill each jar brim full by-and-by,
70  dost thou think that thou wilt always kill outright the robber Fancy lurk-
ing within—or sometimes only maim him and distort him!

---

3     *Morgiana in the Forty Thieves:* in *1,001 Arabian Nights,* the slave girl who killed
a group of thieves by pouring boiling oil in the pots where they were hiding

10.  The teaching philosophy prescribed by the three men in the passage
can be summed up as all of the following EXCEPT

A.   flexible

B.   focused

C.   peremptory

D.   literal

E.   thorough

11.  In lines 3–5, the class is depicted as mostly

A.   soporific

B.   contentious

C.   compliant

D.   inquisitive

E.   brilliant

12.  In lines 9–11, the government official views a "grown woman" as

A.   domestic and subordinate

B.   creative and wild

C.   playful and childlike

D.   surreptitious and traitorous

E.   vicious and cruel

13. In lines 6–20, the government official views Sissy as

    A. rebellious
    B. intelligent
    C. creative
    D. aloof
    E. misguided

14. In lines 6–20, the narrator portrays Sissy as all of the following EXCEPT

    A. modest
    B. polite
    C. sensitive
    D. malleable
    E. discerning

15. In lines 21–22, Thomas Gradgrind is

    A. mulling over the words of the government official
    B. mocking the pompousness of the government official
    C. confirming the instruction given by the government official
    D. attempting to ease Sissy's nervousness
    E. directing Sissy's attention away from the classmates who distract her

16. The word "Fancy" (line 28) is closest in meaning to

    A. belief
    B. imagination
    C. interpretation
    D. whim
    E. interest

17. Which of the following is the best example of the government official's discussion concerning "any object of use or ornament" (lines 29–30)?

    A.   "a carpet having a representation of flowers on it" (lines 1–2)
    B.   "tables and chairs" (line 14)
    C.   "Fact, fact, fact" (line 23)
    D.   "a board of fact" (line 26)
    E.   "the people" (line 27)

18. According to lines 25–39, which of the following images would the government official most likely prefer to see on the wall of his study?

    A.   cats
    B.   octagons
    C.   hedges
    D.   windows
    E.   birds

19. When the government official states, "This is fact. This is taste," (line 39), he is

    A.   correcting himself on the spot
    B.   differentiating between his views and Sissy's
    C.   indicating first the nature of reality, then the aspects of reasoning
    D.   recalling what Sissy has already learned in the classroom
    E.   suggesting that one's sensibilities should be derived from empirical evidence

20. The narrator's observation that "She was very young" (line 40) implies that Sissy is

    A.   ill-suited for school
    B.   too immature for facts
    C.   unready for the government official's lesson
    D.   inattentive and absentminded
    E.   in need of Thomas Gradgrind's discipline

21. What does the word "factory" in line 50 most likely imply?

　　A.　efficiency

　　B.　commercialism

　　C.　homogeny

　　D.　ignorance

　　E.　stamina

22. In the context of lines 48–51, the "pianoforte legs" create an image of

　　A.　musicality

　　B.　reduction

　　C.　sturdiness

　　D.　sophistication

　　E.　suffering

23. The list of subjects in lines 52–55 suggest all of the following EXCEPT

　　A.　thoroughness

　　B.　rigor

　　C.　feeling

　　D.　analysis

　　E.　variety

24. Of the subjects listed in lines 52–55, the one that seems most incongruous with the others is

　　A.　etymology

　　B.　astronomy

　　C.　algebra

　　D.　vocal music

　　E.　drawing from models

25. The observation, "He knew all about the Water Sheds of all the world (whatever they are)" (lines 59–60), seems most likely to come from the point of view of

   A.   the government official
   B.   Thomas Gradgrind
   C.   the children in class
   D.   the Queen of England
   E.   Mr. M'Choakumchild himself

26. Which of the following would NOT be considered true about the statement, "If he had only learnt a little less, how infinitely better he might have taught much more!" (lines 64–65)?

   A.   It implies a kinship with Sissy Jupe.
   B.   It exemplifies antithesis.
   C.   It seems paradoxical.
   D.   It indicates that vast knowledge does not necessarily lead to good teaching.
   E.   It suggests a flaw in the educational philosophy held by the three men.

27. In lines 66–71, all of the following could be true of the *Arabian Nights* allusion EXCEPT THAT

   A.   M'Choakumchild is likened to Morgiana
   B.   the children of the class are analogous to the thieves
   C.   M'Choakumchild's teaching methods are similar to Morgiana's oil
   D.   the narrator's diction has changed while addressing M'Choakumchild
   E.   the narrator implies that M'Choakumchild is unfit as an educator

28. If "Gradgrindism" were an actual word, it would most likely be defined as

   A. a development in 19th century scholasticism arguing that an individual's taste naturally stems from practical reasoning

   B. an absolute adherence to pragmatism without regard for an individual's identity, emotional welfare, or creative spirit

   C. an educational approach based on painstaking training, certification, and flexible standards of student achievement

   D. a method of teaching involving collaboration among team educators, parents, and students

   E. an inquiry-based technique for determining student interest in vocational, liberal, applied and fine arts

**Questions 29–40. Read the following passage carefully before choosing your answers.**

*[In the following dramatic passage taking place in medieval Denmark, Claudius has just inherited the throne from his dead brother. Claudius now speaks to Hamlet, his nephew and son of the dead king.]*

KING CLAUDIUS

'Tis sweet and commendable in your nature, Hamlet,

To give these mourning duties to your father:

But, you must know, your father lost a father;

That father lost, lost his, and the survivor bound

5   In filial obligation for some term

To do obsequious sorrow: but to persever

In obstinate condolement[1] is a course

Of impious stubbornness; 'tis unmanly grief;

It shows a will most incorrect to heaven,

10  A heart unfortified, a mind impatient,

---

   1    *condolement:* acts of mourning

An understanding simple and unschool'd:

For what we know must be and is as common

As any the most vulgar thing to sense,

Why should we in our peevish opposition

15 Take it to heart? Fie! 'tis a fault to heaven,

A fault against the dead, a fault to nature,

To reason most absurd: whose common theme

Is death of fathers, and who still hath cried,

From the first corse[2] till he that died to-day,

20 'This must be so.' We pray you, throw to earth

This unprevailing woe, and think of us

As of a father: for let the world take note,

You are the most immediate to our throne;

And with no less nobility of love

25 Than that which dearest father bears his son,

Do I impart toward you. For your intent

In going back to school in Wittenberg[3],

It is most retrograde to our desire:

And we beseech you, bend you to remain

30 Here, in the cheer and comfort of our eye,

Our chiefest courtier, cousin, and our son.

---

2    *corse:* corpse

3    *Wittenberg:* German college town

29. Claudius' tone in this passage is best described as

    A.   demanding, then resigned

    B.   elevated, then angry

    C.   chastising, then reassuring

    D.   philosophizing, then surrendering

    E.   bemused, then concerned

30. In lines 1–8, Claudius views Hamlet's mourning as

    A. praiseworthy, but overdone
    B. false, but clever
    C. flattering, but useless
    D. naïve, but practical
    E. loving, but crass

31. In the phrase, "That father lost, lost his" (line 4), the first "lost" is

    A. a verb whose subject is "father"
    B. a verb whose subject is "Hamlet"
    C. a modifier for "Hamlet"
    D. a modifier for "father"
    E. a modifier for "Claudius"

32. In lines 6–11, Claudius regards Hamlet's behavior as all of the following EXCEPT

    A. irreverent
    B. dangerous
    C. effeminate
    D. weak
    E. unwise

33. The word "vulgar" in line 13 is closest in meaning to

    A. ordinary
    B. unrefined
    C. indecent
    D. ostentatious
    E. offensive

34. Claudius' exclamation of "Fie!" in line 15 most likely indicates his

    A.   aggravation with his own ineffectiveness

    B.   frustration with death

    C.   grief over the loss of his brother, Hamlet's father

    D.   inability to express himself

    E.   opposition to Hamlet's lugubrious mood

35. According to Claudius, the declaration "This must be so" (line 20) is stated by

    A.   reason, which implies that it is reasonable to accept death's inevitability

    B.   death, which indicates that death has a regal power

    C.   fathers, which suggests that descendants must obey their ancestors

    D.   a "corse," which insinuates that the dead can communicate with the living

    E.   "he," which means that Hamlet's father knows Claudius is right

36. In lines 20–26, Claudius is doing all of the following EXCEPT

    A.   ingratiating himself to Hamlet

    B.   taking on a paternal tone

    C.   keeping his conversation with Hamlet a secret

    D.   making Hamlet an heir

    E.   assuming that while Hamlet mourns, he has little regard for Claudius

37. In lines 26–28, the most likely reason for Claudius' "desire" is that

    A.   Claudius is jealous of Hamlet's freedom

    B.   Hamlet has not yet fulfilled his princely duties in Denmark

    C.   Hamlet needs to be disciplined for his lack of propriety

    D.   Hamlet has not expressed gratitude to Claudius for taking over Denmark

    E.   Claudius wants to see Hamlet happier before the young man goes anywhere

38. In the context of lines 29–31, the word "bend" is closest in meaning to

    A. force
    B. implore
    C. vote
    D. decree
    E. challenge

39. In lines 29–31, Claudius sees himself as which of the following?

    I.   soother
    II.  ruler
    III. father

       A. II only
       B. I & II
       C. I & III
       D. II & III
       E. I, II, & III

40. Which of the following would best sum up Claudius' view of fathers and sons?

    A. Once a father is gone, the son should forget him and move on.
    B. A son should pay more heed to a present father figure than an absent biological father.
    C. The father/son relationship should be built on love and mutual respect.
    D. An emotional son dishonors his father more than an irresponsible son.
    E. An uncle can act as a father if he takes on the personality of that father.

**Questions 41–56. Read the following passage carefully before choosing your answers.**

*[In the following passage, young Victorian gentleman Dorian Gray is watching a performance of Shakespeare's* Romeo and Juliet *starring Sybil Vane, a woman with whom he has recently fallen in love. However, despite the talent she has displayed on previous nights, so far, the first two acts have proceeded dreadfully tonight; Sybil is acting so poorly that Dorian's friends have left the theater despite his protests.]*

A few moments afterwards the footlights flared up and the curtain rose on the third act. Dorian Gray went back to his seat. He looked pale, and proud, and indifferent. The play dragged on, and seemed interminable. Half of the audience went out, tramping in heavy boots and
5  laughing. The whole thing was a fiasco. The last act was played to almost empty benches. The curtain went down on a titter and some groans.

As soon as it was over, Dorian Gray rushed behind the scenes into the greenroom. The girl was standing there alone, with a look of triumph on her face. Her eyes were lit with an exquisite fire. There was
10  a radiance about her. Her parted lips were smiling over some secret of their own.

When he entered, she looked at him, and an expression of infinite joy came over her. "How badly I acted to-night, Dorian!" she cried.

"Horribly!" he answered, gazing at her in amazement. "Horribly! It
15  was dreadful. Are you ill? You have no idea what it was. You have no idea what I suffered."

The girl smiled. "Dorian," she answered, lingering over his name with long-drawn music in her voice, as though it were sweeter than honey to the red petals of her mouth. "Dorian, you should have understood. But
20  you understand now, don't you?"

"Understand what?" he asked, angrily.

"Why I was so bad to-night. Why I shall always be bad. Why I shall never act well again."

He shrugged his shoulders. "You are ill, I suppose. When you are ill
25  you shouldn't act. You make yourself ridiculous. My friends were bored. I was bored."

She seemed not to listen to him. She was transfigured with joy. An ecstasy of happiness dominated her.

"Dorian, Dorian," she cried, "before I knew you, acting was the one
30 reality of my life. It was only in the theatre that I lived. I thought that it was all true. I was Rosalind one night and Portia the other. The joy of Beatrice was my joy, and the sorrows of Cordelia[1] were mine also. I believed in everything. The common people who acted with me seemed to me to be godlike. The painted scenes were my world. I knew nothing
35 but shadows, and I thought them real. You came—oh, my beautiful love!—and you freed my soul from prison. You taught me what reality really is. To-night, for the first time in my life, I saw through the hollowness, the sham, the silliness of the empty pageant in which I had always played. To-night, for the first time, I became conscious that the
40 Romeo was hideous, and old, and painted, that the moonlight in the orchard was false, that the scenery was vulgar, and that the words I had to speak were unreal, were not my words, were not what I wanted to say. You had brought me something higher, something of which all art is but a reflection. You had made me understand what love really is.
45 My love! My love! Prince Charming! Prince of life! I have grown sick of shadows. You are more to me than all art can ever be. What have I to do with the puppets of a play? When I came on to-night, I could not understand how it was that everything had gone from me. I thought that I was going to be wonderful. I found that I could do nothing. Suddenly it
50 dawned on my soul what it all meant. The knowledge was exquisite to me. I heard them hissing, and I smiled. What could they know of love such as ours? Take me away, Dorian—take me away with you, where we can be quite alone. I hate the stage. I might mimic a passion that I do not feel, but I cannot mimic one that burns me like fire. Oh, Dorian,
55 Dorian, you understand now what it signifies? Even if I could do it,

---

1    *"I was Rosalind...Cordelia."* A list of female characters from some of Shakespeare's plays: Rosalind appears in *As You Like It*, Portia in *Julius Caesar*, Beatrice in *Much Ado About Nothing*, and Cordelia in *King Lear*.

it would be profanation for me to play at being in love. You have made me see that."

He flung himself down on the sofa and turned away his face. "You have killed my love," he muttered.

41. The passage portrays Sybil Vane as all of the following EXCEPT

    A.   altered

    B.   enthralled

    C.   unaware

    D.   hesitant

    E.   ebullient

42. The combination of adjectives in the sentence "He looked pale, and proud, and indifferent" (lines 2–3) implies that Dorian

    A.   appreciates Sybil's performance but is starting to be swayed by the audience's opinion

    B.   has been overcome by the magnitude of Shakespeare's tragedy

    C.   cannot abide Sybil's performance, but knows he can help her regain her acting ability

    D.   does not want to be mistaken for an actor in this repertory company

    E.   is aghast at Sybil's performance, but is trying to remain nonchalant

43. What does the description of the audience "tramping in heavy boots" (line 4) suggest?

    A.   The members of the audience are making no attempt to disguise their disdain for Sybil's acting.

    B.   The audience is composed mainly of working class people.

    C.   Dorian is distracted by the audience's fashion *faux pas*.

    D.   The play is taking longer than it should and the audience members are forced to leave.

    E.   In a kind of comically cruel protest, the audience members are marching out in unison.

44. The sentence "The curtain went down on a titter and some groans" (line 6) is an example of

   A.   personification
   B.   hyperbole
   C.   synecdoche
   D.   asyndeton
   E.   indirect metaphor

45. The imagery in lines 7–11 is appropriate for portraying

   A.   the flaming passion that Sybil feels for acting
   B.   the warm appreciation that Sybil has for the audience
   C.   the burning desire that Sybil carries for Dorian
   D.   the scorching hatred that Sybil now has for a career that mocks her
   E.   the new enlightenment that Sybil has received from loving Dorian

46. According to lines 12–23, if she overheard Dorian tell someone that she acted "Horribly," Sybil would most likely respond by saying:

   A.   "Dorian, how could you?"
   B.   "Well, I was distracted by the image of Dorian's face in front of me."
   C.   "Yes, but Dorian has been a terrible influence on me."
   D.   "No, I didn't. I was as convincing as ever."
   E.   "Yes, wasn't it wonderful?"

47. Lines 17–20 feature mixed metaphors that reflect all of the following EXCEPT

   A.   the fact that Sybil and Dorian do not see the current situation in the same way
   B.   the lack of believability in Sybil's acting
   C.   Dorian's misinterpretation of the play
   D.   the scope of Dorian's effect on Sybil
   E.   the sentimentality of Sybil's emotions

48. Lines 24–26 reveal this other reason Dorian has to dislike Sybil's performance:

    A.  He finds her supposed illness repugnant.
    B.  He cannot tolerate her acting when she is apparently ill.
    C.  He is furious that she would try to sabotage her own performance.
    D.  He may be embarrassed that his friends saw the show.
    E.  He may be worried that his friends could refuse to attend the theater with him anymore.

49. The Shakespearean characters listed in lines 31–32 most likely exemplify

    A.  the respect that Sybil has for Shakespeare's plays
    B.  the discernment Sybil has had in choosing dramatic roles
    C.  the facility with which Sybil could believe in false realities
    D.  the type of lover that Sybil wants to be for Dorian
    E.  the characters whose lives now seem more real than Sybil's own

50. When hearing Sybil say, "You taught me what reality really is" (lines 36–37), Dorian would most probably respond by saying:

    A.  "Then let us escape to that reality now, before anyone sees us."
    B.  "Yes, but at too high a cost."
    C.  "I had no idea that my influence on you could be so positive."
    D.  "Then that reality could aid you in making your acting more believable."
    E.  "But is your love for me as real?"

51. The irony that Sybil discovered her "Romeo was hideous, and old, and painted" (lines 39–40) is that, just like her Romeo,

    A.   Dorian will soon no longer fulfill Sybil's image of him as a lover
    B.   Sybil now seems "hideous, and old, and painted" to Dorian
    C.   the audience will betray Sybil by walking out on her
    D.   professional acting will grow "old" for Sybil, who has played too many roles
    E.   the love that Sybil and Dorian share will seem phony to her

52. By calling Dorian "Prince Charming" (line 45), Sybil is

    A.   unwittingly supplying Dorian with the very role he wants to play
    B.   inadvertently devising a reality with Dorian that is just as false as acting
    C.   subconsciously wishing for her acting ability to return
    D.   unsuspectingly casting herself as a sleeping princess who would rather remain numb to reality
    E.   unintentionally elevating him to royal status to justify his criticisms of her

53. The sentence in lines 47–48 ("When I came on...gone from me") demonstrates that Sybil knows she has lost

    A.   Dorian's love
    B.   the audience's respect
    C.   her talent
    D.   her beauty
    E.   her identity

54. The word "exquisite" in line 50 is closest in meaning to

    A.   excruciating
    B.   acute
    C.   fastidious
    D.   tasteful
    E.   beautiful

55. One could most likely infer from lines 57–58 that Dorian

    A.   is tired from Sybil's long performance and needs to rest
    B.   feels that he is losing Sybil's love
    C.   bases his feelings for Sybil more on her talent than on her individuality
    D.   wants Sybil to change back to her former self
    E.   has really had another lover all along

56. Which of the following describe Dorian's realization about his feelings for Sybil by the end of the passage?

    I.    He desires the realization less than Sybil desires hers about reality.
    II.   His realization comes after some denial.
    III.  His realization is more absolute than Sybil's.
    IV.   Both realizations make each character view the other differently.
        A.   I only
        B.   I & II
        C.   I, II, & IV
        D.   II, III, & IV
        E.   I, II, III, & IV

## Section II
## Time: 2 hours

<u>Directions</u>: Section II of this exam requires answers in essay form. The essays will be judged on how well they respond to the questions and the quality of the writing. Write clearly and legibly and check each essay for spelling, punctuation, and other errors. Cross out any errors you make.

## Question 1
**Suggested time:** 40 minutes. This question counts as one-third of your essay score.

<u>Directions:</u> Read the poem below carefully. Then, in a well-written es-
say, explain how the work develops meaning, especially how that meaning can be relevant today, despite the fact that the poem focuses on a
minor character from Greek mythology. You may include—but are not
limited to—imagery, tone and symbolism.

### Tithonus[1]
### by Alfred, Lord Tennyson

The woods decay, the woods decay and fall.
The vapors weep their burthen to the ground,
Man comes and tills the field and lies beneath,
And after many a summer dies the swan
5  Me only cruel immortality
Consumes; I wither slowly in thine arms,
Here at the quiet limit of the world,
A white-hair'd shadow roaming like a dream
The ever-silent spaces of the East,
10  Far-folded mists, and gleaming halls of morn.
Alas! for this gray shadow, once a man—
So glorious in his beauty and thy choice,
Who madest him thy chosen, that he seem'd
To his great heart none other than a God!
15  I ask'd thee, "Give me immortality."
Then didst thou grant mine asking with a smile,
Like wealthy men who care not how they give.
But thy strong Hours indignant work'd their wills,
And beat me down and marr'd and wasted me,
20  And tho' they could not end me, left me maim'd
To dwell in presence of immortal youth,

---

1    *Tithonus:* In Greek mythology, Eos (Roman: Aurora), the goddess of the dawn,
fell in love with the mortal Tithonos (Roman: Tithonus). She gave him eternal life, but
forgot to give him eternal youth, so he lived forever but continued to age.

Immortal age beside immortal youth,

And all I was in ashes. Can thy love

Thy beauty, make amends, tho' even now,

25  Close over us, the silver star, thy guide,

Shines in those tremulous eyes that fill with tears

To hear me? Let me go: take back thy gift:

Why should a man desire in any way

To vary from the kindly race of men,

30  Or pass beyond the goal of ordinance

Where all should pause, as is most meet for all?

A soft air fans the cloud apart; there comes

A glimpse of that dark world where I was born.

Once more the old mysterious glimmer steals

35  From any pure brows, and from thy shoulders pure,

And bosom beating with a heart renew'd.

Thy cheek begins to redden thro' the gloom,

Thy sweet eyes brighten slowly close to mine,

Ere yet they blind the stars, and the wild team

40  Which love thee, yearning for thy yoke, arise,

And shake the darkness from their loosen'd manes,

And beat the twilight into flakes of fire.

Lo! ever thus thou growest beautiful

In silence, then before thine answer given

45  Departest, and thy tears are on my cheek.

Why wilt thou ever scare me with thy tears,

And make me tremble lest a saying learnt,

In days far-off, on that dark earth, be true?

"The Gods themselves cannot recall their gifts."

50  Ay me! ay me! with what another heart

In days far-off, and with what other eyes

I used to watch if I be he that watch'd

The lucid outline forming round thee; saw

The dim curls kindle into sunny rings;

55 Changed with thy mystic change, and felt my blood

Glow with the glow that slowly crimson'd all

Thy presence and thy portals, while I lay,

Mouth, forehead, eyelids, growing dewy-warm

With kisses balmier than half-opening buds

60 Of April, and could hear the lips that kiss'd

Whispering I knew not what of wild and sweet,

Like that strange song I heard Apollo[2] sing,

While Ilion[3] like a mist rose into towers.

Yet hold me not for ever in thine East;

65 How can my nature longer mix with thine?

Coldly thy rosy shadows bathe me, cold

Are all thy lights, and cold my wrinkled feet

Upon thy glimmering thresholds, when the steam

Floats up from those dim fields about the homes

70 Of happy men that have the power to die,

And grassy barrows of the happier dead.

Release me, and restore me to the ground;

Thou seest all things, thou wilt see my grave:

Thou wilt renew thy beauty morn by morn;

75 I earth in earth forget these empty courts,

And thee returning on thy silver wheels.

---

2    *Apollo:* Greek god of the sun and music

3    *Ilion:* another name for Troy, conquered by the Greeks in the ten-year Trojan War

## Question 2

**Suggested time:** 40 minutes. This question counts as one-third of your essay score.

Directions: In the following passage from Amy Tan's *The Joy Luck Club*, Waverly Jong describes a dinner with her fiancé Rich, her parents, and Shoshana, the daughter from her first marriage. Discuss the way the passage develops characterization. You may include, but are not limited to tone, imagery, symbolism, and dramatic irony.

When I offered Rich a fork, he insisted on using the slippery ivory chopsticks. He held them splayed like the knock-kneed legs of an ostrich while picking up a large chunk of sauce-coated eggplant. Halfway between his plate and his open mouth, the chunk fell on his crisp white
5    shirt and then slid into his crotch. It took several minutes to get Shoshana to stop shrieking with laughter.

And then he helped himself to big portions of the shrimp and snow peas, not realizing that he should have taken only a polite spoonful, until everybody had had a morsel.
10    He had declined the sautéed new greens, the tender and expensive leaves of bean plants plucked before the sprouts turn into beans. And Shoshana refused to eat them also, pointing to Rich: "He didn't eat them! He didn't eat them!"

He thought he was being polite by refusing seconds, when he should
15    have followed father's example, who made a big show of taking small portions of seconds, thirds, and even fourths, always saying he could not resist another bite of something or other, and then groaning that he was so full he thought he would burst.

But the worst was when Rich criticized my mother's cooking, and he
20    didn't even know what he had done. As is the Chinese cook's custom, my mother always made disparaging remarks about her own cooking. That night she chose to direct it toward her famous steamed pork and preserved vegetable dish, which she always served with special pride.

"Ai! This dish not salty enough, no flavor," she complained, after tast-
25    ing a small bite. "It is too bad to eat."

This was our family's cue to eat some and proclaim it the best she had ever made. But before we could do so, Rich said, "You know, all it needs is a little soy sauce." And he proceeded to pour a riverful of the salty black stuff on the platter, right before my mother's horrified eyes. And
30    even though I was hoping throughout the dinner that my mother would

somehow see Rich's kindness, his sense of humor and boyish charm, I knew he had failed miserably in her eyes. Rich obviously had had a different opinion on how the evening had gone. When we got home that night, after we put Shoshana to bed, he said modestly, "Well. I
35  think we hit it off *A-o-kay*." He had the look of a dalmatian, panting, loyal, waiting to be petted.

"Uh-hmm," I said. I was putting on an old nightgown, a hint that I was not feeling amorous. I was still shuddering, remembering how Rich had firmly shaken both my parents' hands with the same easy familiar-
40  ity he used with nervous new clients. "Linda, Tim," he said, "we'll see you again soon, I'm sure." My parents' names are Lindo and Tin Jong, and nobody, except a few older family friends, ever calls them by their first names.

"So what did she say when you told her?" And I knew he was refer-
45  ring to our getting married. I had told Rich earlier that I would tell my mother first and let her break the news to my father.

"I never had a chance," I said, which was true. How could I have told my mother I was getting married, when at every possible moment we were alone, she seemed to remark on how much expensive wine
50  Rich liked to drink, or how pale and ill he looked, or how sad Shoshana seemed to be.

Rich was smiling. "How long does it take to say, Mom, Dad, I'm getting married?"

"You don't understand. You don't understand my mother."
55  Rich shook his head. "Whew! You can say that again. Her English is *so* bad."

"Four Directions," from *The Joy Luck Club* by Amy Tan, copyright © 1989 by Amy Tan. Used by permission of G.P. Putnam's Sons, a division of Penguin Group (USA) Inc.

# Question 3

**Suggested time:** 40 minutes. This question counts as one-third of your essay score.

<u>Directions:</u> Often in literature a character or group of characters will undertake a journey to attain a certain goal. However, many times the way in which the characters develop on the journey becomes more important than the goal they seek. In a well-developed essay, select one of the works below, or choose another work of comparable literary merit, and explain how a journey appearing in the work develops characterization.

| | |
|---|---|
| *The Adventures of Huckleberry Finn* | *Moby Dick* |
| *Heart of Darkness* | *Gilgamesh* |
| *The Odyssey* | *The Catcher in the Rye* |
| *The Great Gatsby* | *A Room with a View* |
| *Lolita* | *The Lord of the Rings* |
| *Brave New World* | *The Body* |
| *A Midsummer Night's Dream* | *Their Eyes Were Watching God* |
| *The Grapes of Wrath* | *Don Quixote* |
| *Beowulf* | *The Divine Comedy* |
| *Slaughterhouse-Five* | *The Aeneid* |
| *Henderson the Rain King* | *Candide* |
| *As I Lay Dying* | *Paradise* |
| *A Tale of Two Cities* | *The Awakening* |
| *Frankenstein* | *The Mayor of Casterbridge* |

# Answers and Explanations

PART I

1. **B.** The last two lines of the poem are probably the best evidence for this key. The speaker says, "…every day/we rise new creatures" and "cannot be predicted." Earlier, she also asks the question, "Could I surprise you?" (line 8). Clearly, the priority for her is spontaneity. But could we take that answer a step further and say that she enjoys chaos (C)? Probably not. There is some semblance of order in each "transfiguration" (line 9) she devises, in that they occur regularly: "every day." Chaos then goes too far. A and D imply the opposite of spontaneity. Both consistency and eloquence rely on a predictable kind of order. Finally, the speaker does not seem to be seeking praise (E.). She wants to know if she can "surprise" the addressee, not if he can appreciate her transfigurations.

2. **A.** (Notice in this set that we have two broad introductory questions: unusual, but not unheard of.) According to line 7, the addressee has a "lab." Although technically, a historian (B), a musician (C), a teacher (D), and a doctor (E.) could all use some kind of laboratory, the scientist's occupation associates him most closely with this setting. Furthermore, when the speaker questions whether the addressee would "insist on/keeping a pattern to link every transfiguration" (lines 8–9), she makes him sound like someone who seeks order, rather than a person who is merely reflective, like the historian.

3. **C.** The speaker is purposeful (B) because she is proposing to "catch a sea going fish"; she is on a mission. She is considerate (A) because she is catching the fish "for you" (line 3). She is detailed (D) because she envisions the setting in which she will catch the fish: Palace pier, a place more associated with recreation than fishing. But because she has chosen this fun environment in which to fish, her proposal could also be called lighthearted (E.). C seems like the least likely option because she only

makes her offer hypothetically ("Suppose I took..." [line 1]; she doesn't sound crazed or demanding when offering the fish. Therefore, in this EXCEPT question, we choose the "wrong" answer, or C.

4. **E.** The proposal in lines 4–5 is for the speaker to don goggles and wings (who does that?) and fly into the park. Is such a feat even possible? This proposal is more related to fantasy than reality, so the speaker is indeed being fantastic (E.). Flying through sycamore trees sounds a good deal more active than fishing, so she is not being mellow (D). She is not ruining anything while she flies, so C doesn't work, and both A and B can be eliminated, since they are sharp contrasts to "fantastic."

5. **A.** Lines 6–7 join two very different images: a "planetary strike" (line 6), which must take place on an immense astrophysical scale, and the intrusion of a "flamingo leg" (line 7) coming through a laboratory windowsill. We can now cross out D and E, which inadequately use the words "commonplace" and "bland" to describe these unusual occurrences. There is no reference to age in these images, so C does not make the final cut. Both the planets and the leg are natural, even if the speaker means to refer to her own appendage as the flamingo leg, so B can go. We are left with A, which recognizes how astounding the planetary collision is and how silly a skinny, awkward bird leg can be coming through a window.

6. **D.** Each of the speaker's proposals—the fishing expedition under Palace pier, the flight through the park, the poking of the flamingo leg through the window—is a different kind of transfiguration for her. After all three, the speaker asks if she could surprise the addressee. D therefore makes the most sense. A and B are not viable because they put the focus on the addressee rather than the speaker. We do not have enough information to know if the speaker is frustrated with the addressee or not, or if they have had past disagreements. C and E assume too much, so we can't choose them, either.

7. **B.** D and E are making the same assumptions about the couple that C and E made in Question 6. Again, we do not have enough evidence to prove these options true. As the stanza continues past line 10, the speaker says that all of us are creatures who "cannot be predicted." In other words, there is a randomness about us, and B is proven correct. A refers to something that only the speaker does in the poem; the option is too specific to make sense for the stanza. C is the least likely option because the poem sees the addressee as someone orderly and logical.

8. **D.** Each of the speaker's transfigurations proves how unpredictable a human can be; A holds up. The addressee, however, prefers to see how orderly existence is and the final stanza tries to refute this belief; now B works. Communicating her message to the addressee's "heart" (line 11) implies that the speaker is appealing to his emotions (C). And, since she is now communicating by whispering (line 10) "directly" (line 11), E becomes a possibility. The act of whispering, however, does not automatically indicate a shaming act. Whispering can imply intimacy, a desire to be paid attention to, an attempt to be gentle, or various other states. D is thus the only option that can't be proven outright.

9. **B.** If the speaker wants to emphasize how spontaneous human beings are, a poem with rhyme and meter would not be the best way to convey her message. Free verse, without rhyme or meter, is a more unpredictable type of poetry and is thus more suitable for reflecting our randomness as humans. The slashes also only appear at the end of the poem and in nonstandard spots. As punctuation, they are as unpredictable as the poem's verse form. All signs point to B as the key. A and C sympathize with the addressee's attitude which is better reflected by, say, perfectly punctuated couplets and iambic pentameter. The poem's lines vary in length and the punctuation is occasionally odd, but the sentences follow a fairly normal syntax, so D is unlikely. E comes from a bad place. The option demonstrates the attitude of a frustrated reader who is tired of analyzing the poem. The test would not select a poem that displayed any "lack of craft."

10. **A.** The pedagogy espoused by the three men is focused (B) solely on the acquisition of facts, and as such, is also literal (D). It is peremptory (C) because it does not allow for even the consideration of other ideas. It is demonstrated as thorough (E) when the government official expresses the hope that a "board of fact" will force people to be nothing but factual (line 26). Since this educational philosophy is so rigid and narrow, it cannot be flexible (A).

11. **C.** In these lines, the class has figured out what the right answer tends to be when they are being lectured by the government official, and most of them eagerly supply him with that answer. In other words, they are best characterized as "compliant."

12. **A.** The government official hypothesizes in these lines that Sissy would be engaged in the domestic activity of carpeting her room, but then imagines that if she were married, she would be carpeting the room of her husband instead of her own room, or instead of her husband doing the carpeting himself. Therefore, she is also subordinate to her husband in this instance.

13. **E.** Because Sissy is a pupil who doesn't "get" what the official is trying to teach, because she is someone who embraces "Fancy" instead of its opposite "Fact," she may be interpreted as rebellious (A). However, as he questions her, he does not note any defiance in her, and in fact is "elated" (line 19) when she makes what he thinks is an error in judgment. Since he is using her so good-naturedly as an object lesson, he does not view her as rebellious. Furthermore, the questions that he puts to her make her sound as if she is being silly, or even stupid, certainly not intelligent (B). Her desire for a flowered carpet is certainly fanciful and decorative, but not necessarily creative (C), as she would be hypothetically choosing a pattern for the carpet that already exists. Sissy is also engaged in the questioning, not trying to ignore the official, so D is unlikely. Yet obviously in the eyes of the official, Sissy's desire for floral

flooring is wrongheaded, as he spends lines 6–17 trying to correct her mistaken choices.

14. **D.** Is Sissy modest (A) and polite (B)? Yes, as she speaks quietly and deferentially ("If you please, sir…" [line 13]), and curtsies when the official is done with his interrogation. We could also infer that she is sensitive (C), as she is "fond of flowers" (line 13) and, since she notes that carpet flowers would not really be hurt by heavy boots walking on them, we know that she is mindful of the flowers' welfare. She is also discerning (E) because she knows the difference between a real flower and one appearing in a pattern of carpet. Yet, even though the official may like her to be malleable, we do not see her mind being changed by the official's reasoning; she only curtsies and sits after he is done with her. So, D is the most likely choice for this EXCEPT question.

15. **C.** We do not see Sissy's classmates interacting with her in any way, so we can cross out E first. Since Gradgrind speaks "solemnly" in these lines, not soothingly, we can also draw a line through D. We are further aware from the note above the text that Gradgrind is like the headmaster or principal of the school. He is therefore likely to approve of the educational style being promoted in the classroom, unless we are told otherwise. The uncertainty of A and the contempt of B do not seem right for him, especially if you see that Gradgrind is "much obliged" (line 36) to the official for the introduction of M'Choakumchild, the embodiment of the official's philosophy on education. By repeating the "facts," Gradgrind is in sync with the official.

16. **B.** Imagination has the power to alter reality. That ability is what unnerves the official about Fancy: it doesn't match the facts all the time. To him, flowers belong in a garden; quadrupeds like horses belong in a barn or behind a fence. Neither of these creations of Nature should appear as images in carpet or wallpaper. Thus, Sissy's imagination needs to be obliterated so that she will be a better receptacle for facts.

17. **A.** The official tells Sissy that a person is NOT to have any "object of use or ornament" that would be a "contradiction in fact" (lines 29–30). He has already told her imaginary flower carpet contradicts the reality of flowers, so A is the best choice.

18. **D.** Option A would be the worst choice, because the official has said that quadrupeds of any kind would not be factually found on walls, so cats should not appear as images, either. Since he does not like birds (E) painted on crockery for the same reason, one could extrapolate that he wouldn't like them on walls, either. Hedges (C) might be seen in front of exterior walls, but not along interiors. Octagons (B) may be the least offensive of any of these thus far, yet the shapes are only possibilities for a wall. Option D is the only one that actually belongs on (or in) a wall. Its appearance would be the most closely aligned with fact.

19. **E.** The official is much too sure of himself to be doing any kind of self-correction (A). We can also eliminate B and D because Sissy has not put forth any philosophical discussion about facts, nor do we know whether she has learned what the official wants her to learn. Actually, C could be correct if phrased this way: "indicating first the nature of reality, then the results of reasoning about fact." The official's point is that based on fact, so our "taste" should *come from and reflect* fact. This way of thinking is what makes E correct.

20. **C.** In lines 40–42, the description of Sissy sitting down, fearful of a fact-filled world proves Option C correct. The rest of the options here assume too much or are too generalized.

21. **C.** Factories are certainly commercial structures and may be models for efficiency, but to choose either Option A or B would be to ignore the context in which the factory image appears. The word "same" shows up three times in the sentence that uses the factory metaphor, and therefore suggests that the teachers emerging from this new program have all

been homogenized into identical tools of instruction. Option D is wrong because these trainees' education has helped them avoid ignorance, and E is unlikely, since they are newly "turned" (line 38) and haven't had a chance to work yet.

22. **B.** Pianofortes are musical instruments, but their legs are not their musical parts, so A is suspect. The repetition of the word "same" in these lines dims the likelihood of C and D in favor of B: these would-be educators have been reduced from their original identities by the same educational template. We do not know, however, if they have suffered in this process, so E goes too far.

23. **C.** The list of educational subjects implies thoroughness (A) in its length, rigor (B) and analysis (D) in the substance of its disciplines, variety (E) in its blending of arts and sciences, but nowhere is feeling discussed in the list. These are items to be studied and mastered, not related to or cared for.

24. **D.** Options A, B, and C all fit nicely with the rest of the scientific subjects listed in these lines, so really, we only need look at the two "fine arts" categories: D and E. Of these two, drawing from models is more suitable to the factual model of learning promoted by the official: this is not drawing from imagination, but from a factual, pre-existing form. Only vocal music seems to be the option that could allow for some artistry or creativity.

25. **C.** A watershed is a pivotal moment in history. If M'Choakumchild knows "all about" (line 60) watersheds, then E has just got to be wrong. Moreover, if he is standing in this classroom, approved by the queen's Schedule B, approved by the official who has brought him, and approved by the school's headmaster, then A, B and D would be unlikely as well. Notice, though, that the word "watershed" is divided as "Water Shed," to emphasize the misunderstanding about it. It must be the children of the class who don't know what the teacher is talking about. And we have

further proof that M'Choakumchild can't relate to his students, nor does the program that made him.

26. **A.** The statement is antithetical (B) in its opposition of "less" and "more." It seems paradoxical (C) because the logical assumption would be that if one learns more, he can teach more, or better. However, the passage elsewhere thinks of learners as containers; if this is true, then M'Choakumchild has "filled up" too much on subject matter and left no room for relating to students or teaching beyond the limitations of fact. We can now therefore see the sense of D as well. And if D could be true, then E also must have validity, because the three men believe that fact-focused teaching is the best way to learn. Yet M'Choakumchild is far removed from Sissy, who is less interested in fact and more in Fancy.

27. **B.** In the *Arabian Nights* story, Morgiana pours boiling oil on thieves in large pots and kills them. So, too, M'Choakumchild is going to pour his facts in the children and cruelly kill (or at least maim) their imaginations. If the children were seen as the thieves in this analogy, then the teacher would be killing his students, not just their imaginations.

28. **B.** Based on the way the text has been discussed so far, there is at least one word or phrase in each distracter that makes it wrong: Option A, "naturally" (reasoning has to be forced on the students, as it was with Sissy); Option C, "flexible" (the Gradgrind School is rigid in its curriculum); Option D, "collaboration" (the Gradgrind School is teacher-oriented...students and parents have no say in the curriculum); and Option E, "student interest" (No one teaching at the school cares about validating the students' interests).

29. **C.** From lines 1–20a, Claudius is saying that Hamlet's grief for his father's death is understandable, but much too overstated. To continue in "obsequious sorrow" (line 6) is a sign of "impious stubbornness" (line 8). Hamlet needs to move on, emotionally speaking. Claudius is therefore chastising Hamlet, taking him to task for being too sentimental. Yet in

lines 20b–23, Claudius begins to be reassuring on two counts. The first is that he wants Hamlet to think of him as a father. The second is that he promises Hamlet will be next in line for the throne. Claudius is being demanding, as A would indicate, and does a bit of philosophizing, as D says, yet he resigns himself to nothing, surrenders nothing; it's his way or the highway for Hamlet. Claudius wants Hamlet to get over himself and to stay in Denmark rather than returning to Wittenberg. A less careful reader might be tempted to choose B because of Claudius' lofty blank verse style, but Claudius certainly does not end his speech on an angry note when he refers to Hamlet as a "courtier" and a "son" (line 31); these are compliments to Hamlet. And although Claudius may be bemused (E) by Hamlet's behavior, he is less concerned by the end of the speech than comforting and controlling.

30. **A.** Claudius calls Hamlet's mourning "sweet and commendable" (line 1), so it is praiseworthy, and as we said in our explanation of Question 18, Claudius also calls Hamlet's grief "obstinate," so it is too much. B is probably the least likely answer because Claudius recognizes Hamlet's emotions as genuine. As for C, there is an indication that Hamlet is flattering his father's memory by engaging in "obsequious sorrow," but Claudius never refers to the futility of Hamlet's feelings in lines 1–8, even though one may infer a discussion of grief's uselessness in later lines. Similarly, one may be able to see that Claudius thinks Hamlet's actions are loving but crass (E) later in the passage, just not in lines 1–8. Of course, one might understand in 1–8 that Claudius is subtly calling Hamlet naïve, but collectively, lines 1–20 say that Hamlet is being most impractical in his sorrow, so D is erased.

31. **D.** Occasionally, a grammar question will pop up just to clarify a sentence in a passage, so don't be bothered by the unusual nature of this question. Let's first look at the phrase "That father lost." If D is right, why didn't Claudius just say "That lost father," or "That dead father," since that's really what the phrase means. We will offer two reasons.

First, "That father lost" follows the flow of iambic pentameter in the blank verse of the passage; the stresses or accents go on the even syllables of the phrase (that FA-ther LOST). Second, Claudius is cleverly changing the meaning of the word "lost" from adjective to verb: "That father lost [adjective], lost [verb] his…" He is employing rhetorical strategies to make himself sound clever and therefore more convincing.

32. **B.** If you know the play *Hamlet*, you may be led to think that Claudius views Hamlet as dangerous, but so far in this early passage from the play, Claudius is remaining reserved and has not yet indicated that he thinks his nephew unsafe. But in lines 6–11, is Hamlet irreverent (A)? Yes, as the word "impious" (line 8) suggests. Also in line 8, the word "unmanly" shows that Claudius thinks Hamlet "effeminate" (C). If Hamlet has an "unfortified" heart (line 10), then he is weak (D). And if he has a "simple and unschooled" understanding of the situation (line 11), then he is unwise (E).

33. **A.** Beginning in line 12, the phrase "what we know" refers to death, or more specifically, to the death of fathers. Claudius says that death is a "common" occurrence, so common, in fact that it is the most "vulgar thing to sense." Therefore, the word "vulgar" is synonymous with "common." "Vulgar" these days is associated more with some of the other options you see in Question 22, but here, it is used in an older sense, relating more to "ordinary" than "indecent."

34. **E.** A could not be right here, because Claudius' entire monologue is focused on Hamlet's behavior. The only time Claudius mentions anything about himself occurs after the "Fie!" of line 15. For the same reason, B and C can be eradicated. B may seem possible, but Claudius is not frustrated by death; all along, he has seen it as an ordinary part of life. He is frustrated by Hamlet's overly mournful (E) attitude. The king wants his nephew to "snap out of it."

35. **A.** All we have to do to know that A is right is to trace the sentence back to the subject or "agent" that is speaking the line, "This must be

so." First, the line is not just said, but "cried" as we see in line 18. The one doing this crying is "who" ("who still hath cried"). Next, we need to see to what this "who" refers. The word "and" links the word "who" to the phrase "whose common theme" (line 17; "*whose* common theme/ Is death of fathers and *who* still hath cried…"). Both of these relative pronouns "who" and "whose" refer back to "reason" in line 17. So, not only does reason find our "peevish opposition" (line 14) to death "most absurd" (line 17), but in reacting to our silliness, reason cries out "This [death] must be so."

36. **C.** In lines 20–26, Claudius says that he wants to be like a father to Hamlet—even refers to him as a "son"—(B), and he guarantees that Hamlet will inherit the throne of Denmark (D). Thus, in two ways Claudius is ingratiating himself to his nephew (A). Also, when he tells Hamlet to "throw" his grief "to earth" and to think of Claudius as a parent, one could infer that Claudius believes the following: while Hamlet grieves for his father, he cannot think of anyone else as a paternal figure; however, if Hamlet discards his grief, he can start to have a higher regard for Claudius. Using this reasoning, one could make E viable. However, C is contradicted when Claudius tells the world to "take note" (line 22) that Hamlet will be heir to the crown. Here, the king is making a public declaration of his intent to make Hamlet heir apparent.

37. **E.** Basically, A, B, C, and D make too many assumptions. As king, Claudius would be expected to stay in Denmark, while Hamlet has the freedom to travel abroad; however, Claudius never suggests any jealousy of Hamlet in this monologue (A). Furthermore, Claudius has not named multiple duties that Prince Hamlet must fulfill (B); the king just wants his nephew to hurry up and get over his dad's death. C can't be right because even though the king says that Hamlet is behaving inappropriately, Claudius doesn't say Hamlet's staying in Denmark is a punishment, nor does Claudius express a need for thanks from Hamlet (D). What Claudius *does* say is that while Hamlet remains in the country,

he will be in the "cheer and comfort" of Claudius' eye. This last command offers a way for Hamlet to achieve happiness: to be influenced by Claudius' own high spirits. Perhaps, if Hamlet allows himself to perk up, he could conceivably leave Denmark, but certainly not before.

38. **B.** Before the king has used the word "bend," he has used the term "beseech," which is very much like "implore" (B). A, D, and E all sound too much like bullying. Claudius is trying to cajole Hamlet, telling the young man that by staying in Denmark, he will be around cheerful people. As for C, the option seems much too democratic for a king to use.

39. **E.** If the king wants Hamlet to remain in the "comfort" of Claudius' eye, then Claudius sees himself as a soother ("I"). If he refers to Hamlet as "our chiefest courtier…and our son" (line 31), then these roles make Claudius both king and father ("II" and "III").

40. **B.** If you answered A, you probably just jumped the gun and didn't wait for a more even-handed answer to come along. Not once does Claudius tell Hamlet to forget his father. The king just wants Hamlet to stop the grieving process. By the end of the monologue, Claudius is offering himself as a surrogate parent. So, better to have someone there for you who can act like a parent than to incessantly mourn for the real father who is no longer around. C, D, and E all sound as if they would be good maxims for a son to remember, but Claudius simply hasn't touched on any of them.

41. **D.** Sybil has been altered in two ways. First, she has lost her acting ability. Next, she has made the realization that Dorian's love—or what she thinks is Dorian's love—has caused her to spurn the falseness of acting. Thus, A is applicable. Also, there may be two ways in which she is or has been enthralled (B). On the one hand, the passage shows her as being utterly smitten by Dorian; she is enthralled by her attraction to him. On the other hand, if we think of the word "enthralled" as an antonym for "free," we can look to line 36 of the passage, where Sybil

tells Dorian, "…you freed my soul from prison." Either her false belief in acting has kept her from being free, or, more ironically, she is still enthralled because Dorian's love for her no longer exists. Now, what about C? Is she unaware? Yes. From the way she goes on and on about Dorian's influence over her, we can tell that she is oblivious to Dorian's distaste for her performance. As for E, nothing marks Sybil better than her ebullience. She is bubbling over with joy, not only from her love for Dorian, but also from her new discovery that she no longer wants to act. She is going at this new phase of her life with full force, never once showing any hesitancy, so D is our best option.

42. **E.** From the beginning of the passage to the end, Dorian has absolutely loathed Sybil's Juliet, so A can't be supported. Perhaps B could be true if Dorian found anything in the play that he liked; but he didn't, so B is wrong. C could be right if we saw in the conversation between Dorian and Sybil some advice he gives her for improvement. However, the closest he comes to advice is making excuses for her wooden performance by saying that perhaps she is ill. D is probably the least likely answer, because if he were in the repertory company, wouldn't he probably be on stage, or backstage? Now, let's look at the adjectives in line 3. If one looks proud and indifferent, he wouldn't ordinarily look pale also. A pale face is associated with fright, sickness, or humiliation. So Dorian's pale condition betrays his horror at Sybil's terrible acting, while the pride and indifference on his face are an attempt to remain aloof, to disassociate himself from what is happening on stage. E makes more sense here.

43. **A.** B either relies on a stereotype or makes a big assumption: either working class people are the only ones to wear heavy boots, or Shakespeare is a big draw mainly for working class people. Neither supposition sounds valid, so B is out. C also assumes too much; the passage doesn't indicate what is fashionable in footwear during the Victorian period, so we have no way of knowing whether heavy boots are gauche or not. If the play seems to Dorian to drag on, it does so because the

acting is bad, not necessarily because it is slow. Therefore, D can be laid to rest. Finally, the phrase "tramping out" is not the same as "marching in unison." We thus wave goodbye to E. We can say, however, that tramping is a loud and forceful sound. No one leaving is trying to be quiet as they exit (A), so they either don't care if their dislike of the play is known, or they are purposefully making noise to communicate to the actors that the play is horrid.

44. **C.** If the curtain literally went down on a titter and some groans, these sounds would have to exist on their own, as disembodied entities. Rather, the sounds represent audience members unhappy with the play. The titter and groans are *parts* used to represent the *whole*, and are therefore examples of synecdoche.

45. **E.** If you answered C, you may not have been reading carefully enough. Although it is true that Sybil is ga-ga for Dorian, the images of heat and light that describe her in this paragraph refer to a "triumph" that she has made (line 9). She would not feel that she needs to triumph over Dorian; she is, after all, already in a relationship with him. Instead, what she has conquered is a new attitude, a belief in the falsehood of acting. She later credits this new "enlightenment" (hence the descriptors of "fire" and "radiance" in lines 9–10) to Dorian's influence on her life. With this distinction in mind, we can now understand how wrong A is. We also see that Sybil has no regard for the audience's opinion of her acting. With happiness, she cries out how badly she acted in the play. She knows that there is no reason to be appreciative of the audience members (B). And although she does not want to act again, Sybil feels no resentment toward acting. In fact, she is too taken with her love for Dorian to feel something as strong as "hatred" (D) for her career.

46. **E.** In lines 12–23, Sybil is actually proud of the poor performance she has given. She interprets her atrocious acting as proof of a higher consciousness: the recognition that her true love for Dorian has exposed

acting as a lie. She is happy when she says, "How badly I acted to-night, Dorian!" (line 13). She actually embraces her mediocrity. A and D do not acknowledge her acceptance of her poor skills, while B and C make Sybil sound as if she blames Dorian for what has happened to her. She doesn't blame him; she is grateful.

47. C. First, what exactly are the mixed metaphors in lines 17–20? They pertain to the utterance of the word "Dorian" coming from Sybil's mouth. The sound of the word is compared to music in these lines, then the music quickly becomes honey. We awkwardly move from a sound to a taste, but then the honey falls on the petals of Sybil's mouth; flower petals aren't capable of taste, so again the metaphors are crossing strangely. Is this short-circuiting imagery a sign of the passage's poor construction? Hardly. There can actually be a purpose for the mis-matched metaphors. They can emblemize: 1) the way that Dorian and Sybil have differing opinions about what has just happened on stage (A); 2) the way in which Sybil's unrefined performance did not adequately portray Shakespeare's Juliet (B); 3) the great appeal that Dorian has to Sybil, as his name is compared to music (hearing) and honey (taste) (D); and 4) the overwrought, saccharine feelings Sybil has for Dorian (E). Yet, as much as Dorian disliked the play, he did not misinterpret it (C). He understands *Romeo and Juliet*; he just doesn't think that Sybil's performance in it was believable.

48. **D.** References to Dorian's friends and Sybil's possible illness are both made in these lines, so why does D win out? Let's eliminate the distract-ers first. A isn't plausible because Dorian would actually like to blame Sybil's bad acting on an illness. He isn't repulsed by her supposed sick-ness; rather, he can't stand her lack of talent. For this same reason, B can be thrown out. C assumes that Dorian knows the reason behind Sybil's plummet from genius, yet Dorian has no idea why she would be acting so horrendously. He is fuming in bewildered frustration while she ex-plains herself. So now we are left with D and E, which refer to Dorian's

friends in the audience. E makes assumptions about the future that the passage can't support. D seems more likely, especially when we recall how "proud" Dorian looks in line 3, despite the fact that he is pale. He must be embarrassed by Sybil's acting. But that embarrassment could have been exacerbated by the fact that his friends not only saw the show, but also left before it ended.

49. **C.** Because of the passage footnote, we can immediately eliminate D as an option. We don't know enough about the characters listed to be sure that they are portrayed as lovers in their respective plays (certainly Cordelia is not known this way). If you have been following the explanations thus far, then you know that E can also be knocked down. Sybil has explained to Dorian that she thinks acting lacks authenticity, so these characters would now seem *less* real to her than before. A and B sound like good responses because Shakespeare is such a well-respected writer, but they fail to take into consideration the context in which Sybil has mentioned characters like Rosalind and Portia. In lines 32–33, Sybil says about these characters, "I believed in everything." In other words, she could just as easily believe in Rosalind's situation as Portia's; she moved among characters easily, because she could so easily suspend her disbelief when she played them.

50. **B.** According to Sybil, Dorian's love has helped her understand authentic reality. Yet the cost is that she can no longer act on stage. Dorian is horrified by her decline in skill, so much so that by the end of the passage, he claims that Sybil has killed his love for her. Clearly, the cost of her new knowledge is too much for him.

51. **A.** Throughout the passage, Sybil's love for Dorian seems vast. Even if he stops loving her, she would never call her feelings for him "phony," so E does not hold. D may seem to have some merit because Sybil no longer wants to act; however, she doesn't say that acting has grown old for her, as if she has performed for too much of her life. Instead, she has

recognized how artificial acting is. We know that C does not apply either, because she doesn't seem to mind that the audience has rejected her. She knows her acting is bad, and she is happy, because she now lives with a new awareness of a better reality. B seems least plausible, because even though Sybil's acting may seem "hideous" to Dorian, she has not aged to him, and since he is a big fan of good acting, he may not mind her being painted for stage work. Yet by the close of the passage, we know that Dorian is breaking up with Sybil. Her realization about acting's falsehood has come from Dorian's love, but ironically, the disappearance of her acting talent will also cause the end of that love.

52. **B.** Sybil doesn't like the counterfeit nature of the stage, but when she calls Dorian "Prince Charming," she is hardly grounded in reality. She is exchanging the play *Romeo and Juliet*, which she has just performed, for another fiction: a fairy tale. She doesn't realize how appropriate this twist is. Since Dorian will reject her by the end of the passage, we can see that the only way their love could survive would be as a fairy tale.

53. **C.** Again, Sybil knows that she has acted poorly tonight, but she doesn't mind. In fact, she is happy to have been so amateurish. Her mechanical performance only proves how real her love for Dorian is.

54. **E.** If the epiphany Sybil has had were excruciating (A), it would have been painful to her; yet she delights in her new knowledge. B and C seem wrong because they both are too pointed or finite; by contrast, Sybil's revelation seems to encompass every aspect of her life: her career, her relationships, her identity. D seems to appeal to some aesthetic sensibility; it therefore must be completely opposed to the new authenticity that Sybil is experiencing. In the sentence following line 39, Sybil smiles despite the hissing of the audience. To her, the realization of acting's fabrication is beautiful.

55. **C.** The passage shows Sybil as a woman of deep feeling, of great intellectual and emotional capacity. She obviously adores Dorian, and

wants to spend eternity with him. Yet none of these qualities is enough for Dorian. He is primarily concerned with her acting talent. Once that is gone, he has no feelings for her.

56. **B**. Sybil embraces her new beliefs about acting, but Dorian has not wanted to fall out of love with Sybil, so "I" stands firm. Dorian has tried to attribute Sybil's bad acting to a temporary illness, and then realizes that she is perfectly well, so "II" can also work. Yet Sybil's realization about acting and Dorian's about his feelings both seem complete and un-changing, so "III" sits on shaky ground. "IV" could work for Dorian. He begins the passage embarrassed and dumbfounded about Sybil's acting and ends by realizing the permanence of her change and the dissolving of his feelings for her. However, "IV" does not apply to Sybil; all the way through, she idolizes her man.

## PART II

### Response 1A: The "9" Essay

[Note three important things about this essay. First, although you may be turned off by its focus on prepositions, there's a respectable attempt here to take a fresh and original approach to the topic. Concentrating on a grammatical feature of a text will not necessarily net you a "9," but paying attention to that phrase in the prompt ("You may include—but are not limited to—") can get you to think about the text in unique ways. The second thing to mark is the essay's sophisticated organization. There is no simple chronological run through the text here. The writer is grouping her examples topically, an approach that is more challenging, but more rewarding. Furthermore, the writer's language is sophisticated without being too lofty.

The third thing to note is the author's introduction. She begins gen-erally, but does not stray outside the realm of Greek mythology. She is therefore focused on the text and not rambling on and on about society, or the history of humankind. Every example of text she discusses in her body is related right back to her containment idea, without unnecessarily rehashing the content of her quotations. And her conclusion, which admittedly does end a bit abruptly (no "9" is perfect) refers back to the prompt without quoting it verbatim. This essay is original, thorough, and sophisticated: a true "9."]

Besides Prometheus, there may be no one more contained or restricted in Greek mythology than Tithonus. Tennyson's poem "Tithonus" portrays the character living in the celestial palace of his lover Aurora, where he can look down and catch "A glimpse of that dark world where [he] was born" (line 33), yet this is no comfort for him. Just as his immortality separates him from the Earth, effectively imprisoning him in the Aurora's palace forever, so too, he is serving an ongoing life sentence inside his own decrepit body. Oddly, one aspect of the poem that models this imprisonment is Tithonus' use of prepositional phrases beginning with the word "in," as if he is obsessing about the idea of containment: *in* heaven, away from Earth, and *in* his undying corpse.

One place to start exploring this pattern is his repetition of the phrase "In days far-off." Tithonus recalls that, during this distant time of his long life, he learned a saying: "'The Gods themselves cannot recall their gifts'" (line 49). This maxim is wormwood for him now: not only will he continue to age, but Aurora's tears inform him that she cannot take back the "blessing" of eternal life that has been bestowed on him. In line 51, he again uses the phrase "In days far-off," remembering that, at a more youthful period of his existence, he admired the daily radiance that grew around Aurora as she gathered the morning light. Yet the repetition of "In days far-off" joins this happy memory with the dark reminder of the saying that damns him to rot in heaven forever. The effect is that the "in" phrase reflects the remote containment of his happiness.

Similar "in" phrases foreshadow the misery Tithonus will suffer in the present. When Aurora first takes him as a lover, he sees himself as "none other than a God" (line 14), because he felt glorious "in his beauty" (line 12). He thus begs Aurora for immortality. But his hubris will catch up to him. As the ages pass, he will no longer be glorious "in his beauty," but while his "immortal age" dwells "in presence of immortal youth" he will come to a state where he is all "in ashes" (line 23). At first, the phrase "in his beauty" may have sounded promising, but it only emblemizes how removed Tithonus wants to be from his humanity. The result is that he is not only decaying "in ashes," but also withering "in [Aurora's] arms" (line 6) and held forever "in [her] East" (line 64). Enclosed in these boundaries, he neither truly lives nor dies.

These images of containment establish how inhuman Tithonus has become. He now regrets his request for eternal life and the pride that motivated the request: "Why should a man desire in any way/To vary from a kindly race of men/Or pass beyond the goal of ordinance/Where all should pause…?" (lines 28-31). The phrase "in any way" demonstrates a transition in Tithonus' thinking. He realizes now that he should never have wanted anything beyond his own humanity. The "in any way" regards immortality as the wrong condition for a human being, just as the other "in" phrases have suggested.

The only time an "in" phrase offers comfort for Tithonus occurs when he beseeches Aurora to release him from eternity so that he can be like "happy men that have the power to die" (line 70). He imagines a time when he will return home, when he will "earth in earth forget these empty courts" (line 75). This last kind of containment seems more fitting for Tithonus. In the confines of Aurora's arms, imprisoned in her East, he is a desiccated man, out of place with eternal youth. Yet, "in earth," he would be content, because as he notes, he himself is made of earth.

Tithonus's story is a cautionary tale for those who will not be content with the flaws and finiteness of the human race. Once we seek the means to extend our lives chemically, mechanically, or artistically, we subject ourselves to the irony of losing the very qualities that make us human. And once we embrace immortality, there may be no turning back. As Tennyson's poem ends, Tithonus is only wishing for his life to end. Aurora may not be able to grant him this last request to become mortal. Just as he is contained in a bodily prison, so she is bound never to recall her "gift."

### Response 1B: The "6" Essay (words in bold indicate grammar, mechanics, and usage problems)

[This essay has all the earmarks of a "5": it doesn't do much in the intro except rehash the prompt, it develops with a standard organization, it begins to show signs of grammar and usage problems, and it selects unsurprising aspects of the text to discuss. However, the connections that the writer is able to make within the text, especially differentiating between Aurora's warmth and the steam of the "dim fields," requires some sophistication. An AP reader would notice these features and reward this writer with a "6." Notice, though, that each successive example in the discussion receives less and less support. The writer seems to be running out of steam.]

In Tennyson's poem **Tithonus** a mortal man wails about his unfortunate state. He will never die, but he will always grow old. Even though he is a minor character from mythology, his situation can be a lesson to any person from any time. In the poem, images of temperature, a lamenting tone, and the symbol of the East all help develop the idea that humans should never wish for more **then** they have.

First, images of temperature show how out of place Tithonus is. Every morning, he says, the goddess of the dawn's "dim curls kindle into sunny rings" (line 54). He associates her beauty with warmth. And when he was younger, he was part of that warmth. His blood "Glowed with the glow that slowly crimson'd all" (line 56). But now that he is old, the rosy shadows of dawn bathe him "Coldly" (line 66). It isn't that the goddess doesn't love him anymore, but her light and warmth don't work on Tithonus because he is so old. He is like the old man in the nursing home who can never get warm in winter even though he piles twelve blankets on top of him. What is ironic is that the only warmness that he thinks would have any **affect** on him would be from the earth: "when the steam/Floats up from those dim fields about the homes" (lines 68–69). This shows how badly he wants to become a human again.

Second, Tithonus uses a lamenting tone. Words and phrases like "The woods decay" (line 1), "The vapors weep," "summer dies" (line 4), "I was in ashes" (line 23), and "cold my wrinkled feet" (line 67) show how sad Tithonus is to keep on aging and never die. In fact, his lamenting is so strong that he can actually get the goddess to cry herself: "...thy tears are on my cheek" (line 45). But even though she is sad for him, she can't stay. Her horses are ready to "beat the twilight into flakes of fire." He will stay in the palace, but she will get the day ready. They are separate from each other just like she is beautiful and he is withered like a raisin.

Third, the symbol of the East is a big factor in this poem. For Tithonus, the East is **filed** with "ever-silent spaces" (line 9). It is a place where he is held "for ever" (line 64) like a prison. The East is where the dawn is located, but she gets to ride out in the sky with her team of horses. Tithonus is trapped there.

All of these factors show that one should not wish for more than he can handle. When Tithonus first met the goddess, he wanted her to make him immortal. Now, he wants to take that request back. If he had just been happy with what he already had, he wouldn't be wasting away on the floor of the goddess's palace. Instead, he could be resting comfortably in the earth, dead but happy.

## Response 1C: The "3" Essay (by now, grammar, mechanics, and usage problems should seem obvious)

[This essay does not quite reach the level of a "4" because it only selects two elements of the text for discussion, and treats them in a cursory, unsophisticated manner. But it is superior in development compared to a "2." There is an attempt here to see what different ideas could come from the imagery of the poem and the poem's symbols.]

Throughout time, people have lived and died. Tithonus is not one of those people. He would like to die, but he can't. In this poem, Tithonus uses imagery and symbols to make it clear that he wants to die.

The first image is of the woods decaying (line 1). The second is of the weeping vapors. The woods are like Tithonuses body. It is decaying. The vapors are like his sadness, like he is crying.

The next image is that Tithonus is cold. He is cold even when she pours light on him. He wants to die, but she wont let him. She cries because he is so ungreatful for his eternal life. So she leaves him on horseback.

Then there are the symbols. One symbol is the dark world. Tithonus calls the earth dark two times, in lines 33 and 69. But darkness doesn't mean evil. What darkness really is is that the earth is too far away for him to remember it. All he knows now is that he lives in the place of a godess and is miserable. If he could just die, then he would be happy.

When we want what we can't have, we are unhappy. Then when we get what we want at long last, we are still unhappy. If Tithonus finally dies in the ground, he probably still won't be happy.

### Response 2A: The "7" Essay

[In AP lingo, this essay is both persuasive and (mostly) mature. It does slip into an occasionally informal tone that seems inconsistent with the rest of the response. However, the important thing to remember about this "7" is that it does not see Rich as one-dimensional character. He is not just a buffoon who makes an uncomfortable night even more awkward; the response notes that he is trying to be a good dinner guest. Allowing this complexity in the character drives the response up past a "5" or "6." What prevents it from sailing into the "8–9" range is not only its tonal slips, but its simplistic conclusion. It falls into easy predictions and assurances rather than taking the high road and perhaps noticing that Waverly is partially to blame for Rich's failures at dinner.]

In Amy Tan's *The Joy Luck Club*, Rich is Waverly's Anglo fiancé. He is portrayed as a likable, charming young man who is eager to please those around him, but his absolute cluelessness prevents him from being appreciated the way that he wants. At the awkward dinner given by Waverly's parents, Rich never misses an opportunity to make himself look bad. The only problem is that he doesn't know what a doofus he is being.

His first clue should have come from Waverly's sleeping attire: "I was putting on an old nightgown, a hint that I was not feeling amorous" (lines 37–38). But how could she be in the mood after that dinner? Rich has mispronounced her parents' names as Linda (for Lindo) and Tim (for Tin). He has been overly familiar when the occasion called for formality. Above all, he has insulted Mrs. Jong's steamed pork by prescribing soy sauce for it when she was complaining about its lack of saltiness. Despite these missteps, Rich feels as though the evening went swimmingly: "'Well. I think we hit it off A-o-kay'" (lines 34–35). Gently, Waverly tries to hint that he is misguided. She tells him that she hasn't revealed their engagement to her mother, and then offers her reason why: "You don't understand my mother" (line 54). On the one hand, this could be an indication of the difficulty in delivering such weighty news, that one has to do so delicately. On the other hand, Waverly could be saying that Rich's obliviousness to her family's traditions made it too uncomfortable to admit to her mother that Waverly is intending to marry this man. Yet Rich remains in the dark. When Waverly tells him that he does not understand her mother, he replies "Whew! You can say that again. Her English is so bad" (lines 55–56). He reduces Waverly's concern to a matter of a language barrier.

But Rich is really a good-hearted guy who tries to ingratiate himself. He refuses a fork at dinner and attempts to eat with chopsticks…badly. Yet he is moving out of his comfort zone to fit in with his environment. Cheerfully, he heaps big portions onto his plate. His message is that the food looks good and he wants to eat lots of it. But then he refuses seconds and thinks by doing so he is being polite and restrained. His heart is in the right place, but he doesn't have the experience or the sensitivity to pull the evening off. In spite of Rich's goofs, Waverly still tries to be supportive: "I was hoping throughout the dinner that my mother would somehow see Rich's kindness, his sense of humor and boyish charm" (lines 30–31). But no luck. Lindo Jong's eyes betray the scorn she has for Rich. Her comments about everything from his choice of wine to his skinny frame announce her disapproval of Rich.

Waverly has not selected a bad man for her life mate, just an ignorant one. There are bound to be difficulties when two people decide to make a lifelong commitment to each other, but Waverly and Rich's problems are bigger because he is marrying into a culture of which he knows next to nothing. It is possible that these tough patches will be smoothed over during future family dinners, but only time will tell.

### Response 2B: The "4" Essay (conventional errors in bold type)

[The judgmental tone in this response, coupled with its lack of direct quotes, keeps it from being the plausible, competent "5." It is better than a "3," however, because it does provide some insight into Waverly's responsibility for Rich's failures at dinner. And its humorous tone shows the student's comfort with the writing process.]

The problem with Rich is that he needs to find a new girlfriend. In this passage, he makes **alot of** mistakes, **its** true, but at the end of the day, he is trying his hardest to make sure that he fits in well with his future **inlaws**. Waverly needs to cut him some slack.

First of all, Rich is trying to eat with chopsticks. He doesn't even use an American fork when he is eating his dinner with the Jongs. Next, he is putting **alot of** food on his plate and pretending that he likes Mrs. Jong's cooking. Then, when he leaves, he shakes hands with the Jongs and says he will see them again soon. Basically, he is doing what any good guest would do. Being polite and chatting up the parents. When he says the night went A-OK, he was doing his best to make it that way.

But Waverly isn't impressed. She puts on a nightgown that isn't sexy just to try to tell him how wrong he was. But Rich doesn't take the hint, and that's the whole problem.

Waverly is trying to **comunicate** with Rich by using hints. She acts like he is supposed to know what all the rules of her family are. When Mrs. Jong insults her own cooking, how is Rich **suppost** to know that he should say, "Oh, no! This is great! I love Chinese food!" Waverly expects

Rich to look at her dad to know how to act at the table, but she never told Rich that rule.

**There** relationship is doomed. **Not because they are mixed races, but because Waverly doesn't know how to make her feelings clear**. The next place that Waverly and Rich should go to is a marriage **counciler**, but after that, they should not stop at her parents for dinner. The drive-thru would be safer.

### Response 3A: The "7" Essay

[This essay has some solid analysis. Its examples are valid and relevant to the prompt and to its own thesis. On the down side, there are some slips in tone. The references to the "guilt trip" and Twain "pulling a fast one" are amusing, but inconsistent with the rest of the essay's attitude. Furthermore, the conclusion is probably a bit oversimplified. Still, the body develops clearly and consistently.]

In Mark Twain's *Huckleberry Finn*, the title character and his slave friend Jim head down the Mississippi on a makeshift raft. They are taking this journey to gain freedom: Huck from his abusive father, Pap, and Jim from his white owners. However, every time they touch land, a complication arises to send them further down river. This makes their trip even more dangerous. The farther south they travel, the more severe the laws about slavery. Although he never intended to be in this predicament, Huck has to face a choice: whether or not to turn his friend Jim in to the authorities. The final decision that the boy makes says a lot about his character.

The first time that Huck considers betraying Jim, he leaves his friend on the raft to address two men on a boat who are curious about Huck's raft passenger. At first, bothered by his conscience which tells him to do the right thing, Huck is ready to confess to them that the raft harbors a runaway slave. But Jim seems to sense Huck's intent and calls out to him that Jim is grateful for "ol' Huck's" help and friendship, that he doesn't know what he would have done without Huck. In other words, Jim lays it on thick. Huck thought he was just sailing down the Ole Miss; he didn't realize he was taking a guilt trip, too. As the boy nears the two men, he makes up a story about the raft passenger being his father, infected with smallpox. Of course, the men steer clear of the raft and Jim is safe for now. Huck is torn in moments like these. On the one hand, the conscience that his society has given him tells him that he should obey the law and turn Jim in. But his more authentic, personal conscience is telling him to be loyal to his friend and keep him safe.

The pair wind up about as far south as they will go when Jim is captured and taken to the Phelps' farm. As luck would have it, Sally and Silas Phelps are the aunt and uncle of Huck's friend Tom Sawyer, and they mistake Huck for Tom. Tom arrives later and gleefully takes on the role of his older brother Sid. Here, we see how differently motivated Tom and Huck are. Tom loves adventure, reads about it, romanticizes it, tries to make every aspect of his life sound like a French novel. He wants to turn the freeing of Jim into an elaborate game. Huck, on the other hand, is thrown into adventure out of necessity. He has a dark night of the soul trying to figure out whether to free Jim or not, until he finally decides that if helping his friend is morally wrong, okay, then, he'll "go to hell." After all Huck has been through with Jim, Tom winds up looking a little silly in the end and we sympathize with Huck.

Then Twain pulls a fast one. At the end of the novel, we find out that Jim didn't have to escape to freedom. His owner, Miss Watson, has died, and has granted Jim his freedom in her will. His journey south, his suffering, his imprisonment, and the humiliating games that Tom Sawyer put him through were pointless. Then it's Huck's turn to be surprised. Jim admits that one night when they were exploring a house floating down the river, the corpse they spied inside was Huck's Pap. So Huck didn't have to be on the run, either. But if neither of them had taken the journey, they would never have become such close friends, More importantly, the journey was necessary for Huck to develop a conscience that was truly his own, and not one fabricated by the flawed society in which he lived.

## Response 3B: The "4" Essay (words in bold indicate grammar, mechanics, and usage problems)

[This essay could have been a "5" for one or two reasons. First, there is a rudimentary thesis in the introduction that is never really abandoned in the body. Second, each example, though a simplified character sketch, does tie in to the thesis. What sends it down to the level of the "4," though, is its unsophisticated, nonstandard syntax, compounded by textual inaccuracies (Lettuce is a fruit? Bananas grew in 1930s California?) and repetitive points about Tom.]

John **Stinebeck** wrote the great novel **"The Grapes of Wrath" in** the early part of the 20th century during the **depression and the dust bowl**. The Joad family can't get any work, because they are **Oakies**, so they head to **Cali** to try to get some work picking grapes and other fruits such as cherries, **lettuce and bananas**. Along the way they learn about life's hardships, but they also learn to love each other and take care of **there** fellow human beings.

Tom Joad is an ex-murderer, but he is still a good man. He meets up with Jim Casy, who has the same initials as Jesus Christ and makes sacrifices for Tom just like Jesus would. For instance, he covers for Tom when Tom fights an unfair deputy. Then, when Jim gets himself killed during a strike, Tom kills the man who killed Jim. Now, Tom has to run away again, but he has learned something on this journey: he promises his Ma that wherever he sees injustice or wrong, he will follow up on it, and be a kind of lawman but with the training of life and hardship.

Ma is the cement of the family. During the whole trip out **west**, she keeps everybody together, keeping the peace and telling everyone how important family and love are. When the corporations treat **everbody** in the family and in the camp unfairly, Ma reminds them that they have to stick together. Tom doesn't want to **dissapoint** her, but he can't help it. He knows that she will worry about him. That's why he makes her the promise to look out for **opressed** people everywhere.

The book ends with a tragedy and then some hope. Rose of Sharon has been pregnant for a long time, but she has a stillborn baby. There is a man in **there** camp who is starving and **to** weak to eat solid food, so Rose of Sharon feeds him from her own breast milk, "the milk of human **kindness**". This last scene makes it seem like a lesson for all of us. We should not be greedy, but instead look out for one another. The journey that the Joads took out **west** made this lesson possible.

# About the Author

**Tony Armstrong** has taught English at North Central High School in Indianapolis, Indiana, since 1990. He is a former AP test reader and the author of Kaplan's study guide for the SAT Subject Test: Literature. He has also contributed to McGraw-Hill's CD-ROM series and the Shakespeare Podclass by authoring the *Macbeth* guide and coauthoring the *Romeo and Juliet* guide with Jane Mallison.

# Also Available

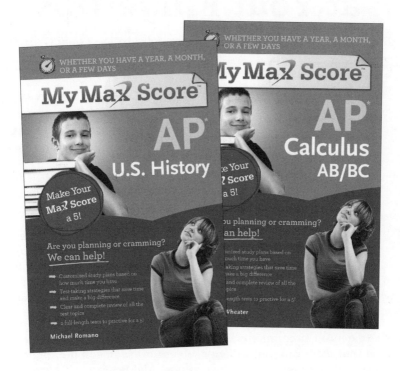

**My Max Score AP U.S. History**
by Michael Romano • 978-1-4022-4310-3

**My Max Score AP English Language and Composition**
by Jocelyn Sisson • 978-1-4022-4312-7

**My Max Score AP Calculus AB/BC**
by Carolyn Wheater • 978-1-4022-4313-4

**My Max Score AP U.S. Government & Politics**
by Del Franz • 978-1-4022-4314-1

$14.99 U.S./ $17.99 CAN/ £9.99 UK

To download additional AP practice tests and learn more about My Max Score, visit mymaxscore.com.

# Online Test Prep at Your Fingertips

*Based on the Strategies and Refreshers of Dr. Gary Gruber.*

**Discover the areas you need to improve and learn proven strategies to maximize your score**

MyMaxScore is a truly innovative program that will revolutionize how students prepare for standardized tests. It's simply the best SAT/ACT prep solution out there! Each student receives an individualized experience focusing specifically on areas in which he/she is weak and spends less time on areas that have already been mastered.

Other test prep programs claim to offer truly personalized prep. The truth is that most programs diagnose your areas needing improvement one time—at the beginning of the course. MyMaxScore offers so much more than that—it actually adapts to your strengths and weaknesses after EVERY practice question! The program continually monitors your progress and serves up questions only in the areas you need to improve.

## Online SAT/ACT prep adapts to you continuously

- ✔ How you answer determines what you study
- ✔ Focus remains on improving unique weaknesses
- ✔ Reports your progress at every step in real time
- ✔ No driving to classes. No more wasted Saturdays.
- ✔ 30 minutes a day
- ✔ Increase confidence. Raise scores.

**Sign up for a FREE Trial**

**Go to MyMaxScore.com today to learn more about how you can max your score!**

# Essentials from
# Dr. Gary Gruber
## and the creators of My Max Score

*"Gruber can ring the bell on any number
of standardized exams."*
—*Chicago Tribune*

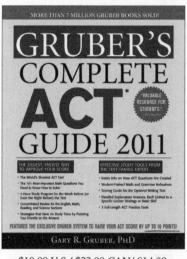

$19.99 U.S./ $23.99 CAN/ £14.99
978-1-4022-4307-3

$19.99 U.S./ $23.99 CAN/ £10.99
978-1-4022-3777-5

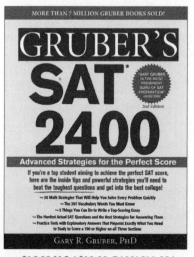

$16.99 U.S./ $19.99 CAN/ £11.99
978-1-4022-4308-0

$13.99 U.S./ $16.99 CAN/ £7.99
978-1-4022-3859-8

"Gruber's methods make the questions
seem amazingly simple to solve."
—*Library Journal*

"Gary Gruber is the leading expert on the SAT."
—*Houston Chronicle*

$14.99 U.S./ $15.99 CAN/ £7.99
978-1-4022-1846-0

$14.99 U.S./ $15.99 CAN/ £7.99
978-1-4022-1847-7

$14.99 U.S./ $15.99 CAN/ £7.99
978-1-4022-1848-4

$12.99 U.S./ $15.99 CAN/ £6.99
978-1-4022-2010-4